MAKING A FORTUNE *QUICKLY* ·IN· FIX-UP PROPERTIES

Andrew James McLean

CB
CONTEMPORARY BOOKS

Library of Congress Cataloging-in-Publication Data

McLean, Andrew James.
Making a fortune quickly in fix-up properties : learn how to locate, finance, improve and sell undervalued real estate for profit / Andrew James McLean..
p. cm.
Includes index.
ISBN 0-8092-4839-5
1. Real estate investment—United States. 2. Dwellings—United States—Remodeling. 3. House buying—United States. 4. House selling—United States. 5. Dwellings—Renovation. I. Title.
HD255.M32 1995
332.63'243—dc20 95-22784
CIP

11 12 13 14 15 16 17 18 19 BKM BKM 0 9 8 7 6 5 4 3 2

Published by Contemporary Books
A division of NTC/Contemporary Publishing Group, Inc.
4255 West Touhy Avenue, Lincolnwood (Chicago), Illinois 60712-1975 U.S.A.

Printed in the United States of America
International Standard Book Number: 0-8092-4839-5

Contents

Author's Note

In writing this book, I have attempted to give sound advice in strategy and procedure for real estate investment. By no means am I rendering legal, accounting, or other professional service. While the procedures offered will likely work throughout the United States, the reader should become familiar with variations in local laws and customs.

Half the states use a mortgage as a security instrument, while the other half use a deed of trust. Thus, it is impossible in a book of this nature to set down standards of practice applicable everywhere. Although the terms are similar, laws regarding foreclosure and real estate vary somewhat, so it is sound judgment to consult a trusted real estate attorney or tax professional to answer specific questions.

For simplicity, the text uses the term *mortgage*, instead of continually describing both it and a deed of trust. For all practical purposes, these instruments are similar, the only major difference being how they are enforced during foreclosure proceedings.

Note: The author has used the masculine pronouns to avoid awkwardness and in no way wishes to slight female readers.

Introduction

WHY READ THIS BOOK?

You need real estate. You need protection from excessive income taxes and the crippling effects of inflation. You need additional income and a lucrative way to develop financial security for you and your family. Investment in real estate offers you all this—and much more!

Let's face it, it's tough trying to be rich, especially while working for someone else. However, having a full-time job is important, but only to get you started at investing in real estate. Your present job can be a springboard to financing your next investments. Once you have developed numerous income-producing properties, then you can consider becoming a full-time investor.

You don't need much to get started. Sometimes you can buy with no money down, and often you need just a few thousand dollars. You don't need a college degree or a real estate license; you don't even need good credit. What you do need is motivation, patience, and the time to study the material presented to you in this book.

What I have prepared for you is a general all-around handbook that encompasses some basic and some new investment techniques you can use during your spare time. You won't need any other books, because this book has everything you need, from what to look for, how to purchase it, how to fix it up, how to rent it out or sell it, and how to manage all your holdings. It includes terminology, examples, and knowledge gained from firsthand experience.

Our efforts will be concentrated on the best opportunities for profit: fix-up properties. A fix-up property, or fixer-upper, is a home in disrepair which can be purchased at a bargain price, refurbished to create value through improvement, and sold at a profit. Skip properties already in good condition; they command top-dollar prices in the real estate marketplace. The key, then, is the creation of value. You have to be able to look at a property in disrepair, determine the cost to put it at peak market value, and purchase it at a price low enough that it will later sell at a substantial profit.

One of the money-making techniques featured in this book is the lease-option. I have been experimenting with this concept over the past five years and found it to be the most profitable way for the small investor to get the most for his money. Through a lease-option, you can avoid many of the pitfalls associated with conventional financing methods.

The contents of this book will help any investor, big or small. Lease-option is a theory that is sound—it's been tested, and the tax advantages and the extra earnings of selling on installment will astound you. I suggest that you glance over a few chapters. If you are entirely new to real estate, familiarize yourself with the terminology in the glossary and then thoroughly read the entire book.

These concepts have been tested and they work. All that is needed from you is to study the material, then implement the concepts. Within a short time you'll have earned yourself a handsome portfolio of income-producing real estate.

WHY REAL ESTATE?

If you take $10,000 and bury it under the floor, in a year it will probably be worth less than $9,400 due to an average rate of inflation of 6%. If you put it in a savings account, it will probably be worth just about $10,000, and no more.

Financially speaking, you need protection against inflation in order to survive. Inflation is moving so fast that, if you have your money in savings, the interest you earn will hardly keep pace; even worse, you have to pay taxes on that interest. What this means, effectively, is that next year your money will be worth no more than it was worth this year. It will not grow. The dollars will increase, but they will be worth much less.

The outlook is a little better for blue-chip stocks. There are minor tax advantages here, and a higher growth rate than in a savings account. If you invest in stocks or bonds, you will show some profit, but not a lot.

Now, I know you've heard of the fortunes made in the stock market. More correctly, many fortunes have been made and lost in the stock market. The broad fluctuations in stock prices are unpredictable and uncontrollable for the average investor. Highly experienced stock traders often make money. But even the experts lose at this game, and for the average investor, stock trading is about as sensible as rolling dice. It may be fun for a game, but you don't want to stake your entire life on the chance of crapping out.

Like stocks, precious metals, such as gold and silver, experience erratic fluctuations in price movement. The value of metals may or may not appreciate over the years. Further, there is the added risk of storing and protecting your precious hoard. Except for a few "insiders," gold and silver are only modestly profitable investments at best. Certainly they are not the path to riches.

Even in the most conservative sense, even without the promise of giant profits, real estate remains the safest, surest form of investment. During the Great Depression, when all forms of assets were either wiped out or substantially devalued, the owners of real property sustained the least damage.

Real estate has permanent value. Its supply is limited, but its demand is unlimited. In an ever-expanding world, the useful life of real property stays constant, the supply diminishes . . . while the demand goes up and up.

The true value to you, as an investor, comes from the unparalleled permanence of real property compared to all other forms of investment and ownership. Permanence and guaranteed demand mean that, with real estate (and only real estate), it is possible to borrow up to 100 percent of the purchase price of a property—and sometimes even more!

You must understand what this means to you personally. It means that if you pay a small down payment and take out a mortgage for the balance owing, the value of your purchase will grow much faster than the rate of inflation, while the size of your loan diminishes.

In most cases you will be able to obtain 90 percent financing by taking out more than one loan. This means that a $10,000 cash investment could purchase $100,000 in real estate, in which case you would owe $90,000 in mortgages for the balance. As time goes by, the loan balance on the mortgages decreases, and the overall value of the property continues to increase. You have only a small equity investment in the property, and your lenders' interest is much bigger. But because you own the property and do not share the profits with the lenders, you receive all the profits when the property appreciates.

The use of a down payment to purchase property worth much, much more is called *leverage*. The principle of leverage gives your investment dollar anywhere from five to ten times or more its original purchasing power.

Millionaires, billionaires, blue-chip corporations, and successful real estate investors alike, all use this lucrative and powerful tool of leverage when investing their capital. Every time you make a down payment and borrow the balance, you are using leverage. The less you put toward the down payment, the more leverage you are using. Maximum leverage, then, would be borrowing 100 percent of the purchase price; paying all cash without a loan would represent the use of zero leverage.

The more you borrow, the higher your rate of return will be on invested capital. (See Chapter 2 for an explanation.) The greater the inflation rate, the more your property appreciates and the more you will make by using leverage.

On the following pages you will find a Comparative Investment Analysis which shows average rates of return on common investments, including three forms of real estate investment. The effects of taxes, inflation, and appreciation are shown for each form of investment (savings account, bonds, stocks, and real estate). The result is the after-tax return on investment (total yield). The total yield (bottom line) is based on an initial $10,000 input for a term of one year.

Notice that the total yield for a savings account is −2.33 percent, primarily due to the effects of income tax and inflation. In other words, at the end of one year, a $10,000 investment in a savings account would actually be worth 2.33 percent less than what you started with. Notice also the dramatic difference in yields under the real estate columns. The yield for real estate using 10 percent down is more than double that using 20 percent down. The reason for this is the powerful tool of leverage.

GETTING STARTED: SETTING ATTAINABLE GOALS

Does this sound like you?

- Day after day you face bumper-to-bumper rush-hour traffic.
- You work too much for too little pay.
- You're tired of a job without a future.
- You're paying too much in income taxes.

Comparative Investment Analysis

	Fixed Yield		Securities	
	Savings accounts	Second mortgages	AAA municipal bonds	Blue-chip stocks
Market value	$10,000	$10,000	$10,000	$10,000
A. Less loan	0	0	0	0
B. = equity	$10,000	$10,000	$10,000	$10,000
C. Gross income	525	1,000	510	420
D. Less expenses	0	0	0	0
E. = net op. income	525	1,000	510	420
F. Yield on mkt. value	5.25%	10%	5.1%	4.2%
G. Less loan paymts.	0	0	0	0
H. Cash flow	525	1,000	510	420
I. Yield on equity	5.25%	10%	5.1%	4.2%
J. Income tax + or − 30%	−158	−300	0	−126
K. Net spendable income	367	700	510	294
L. Yield on equity	3.67%	7%	5.1%	2.94%
M. Plus appreciation	0	0	0	400
N. Net spendable + appreciation	367	700	510	694
O. Less inflation (6%)	−600	−600	−600	−600
P. = net appreciation	−233	100	−90	94
Q. Plus equity buildup	0	0	0	0
R. Total return	−233	100	−90	94
S. Total yield	−2.33%	1%	−9%	.94%

Note: Gross incomes are based on average returns for these forms of investment. Income tax rate based on a 30% average.

Comparative Investment Analysis (cont.)

	Real Estate		
	100% cash free and clear	20% down 80% loan	10% down 90% loan
Market value	$10,000	$50,000	$100,000
A. Less loan	0	−40,000	−90,000
B. = equity	$10,000	$10,000	$10,000
C. Gross income	1,400	7,100	14,200
D. Less expenses	−600	−2,800	−5,600
E. = net op. income	800	4,300	8,600
F. Yield on mkt. value	8%	8.6%	8.6%
G. Less loan paymts.	0	−4,030	−8,060
H. Cash flow	800	270	540
I. Yield on equity	8%	2.7%	5.4%
J. Income tax + or − 30%	−96	330	660
K. Net spendable income	704	600	1,200
L. Yield on equity	7.04%	6%	12%
M. Plus appreciation	1,000	5,000	10,000
N. Net spendable + appreciation	1,704	5,600	11,200
O. Less inflation (6%)	−600	−600	−600
P. = net appreciation	1,104	5,000	10,600
Q. Plus equity buildup	0	370	320
R. Total return	1,104	5,370	10,920
S. Total yield	11.04%	53.7%	109.2%

Note: Gross income based on an average of 7 times gross income for a purchase price. Appreciation is based on an average of 10% annually, yield is determined by deciding total return by equity.
Income tax is figured on tax shelter benefit of depreciation and is on property income. Income tax rate is based on a 30% average.

- You receive only two weeks of vacation in return for an entire year of hard labor.

If in fact that is you, isn't it time you did something about it? You can, because the opportunities are there. All you have to do is draft a plan and implement the concepts you are about to learn in this book.

The great self-made financial empires all began with some form of investment. Rome wasn't built in a day . . . and if you plan to build an empire, you first have to learn how it can be done, then act. You have taken the first step by purchasing this book. Read it thoroughly, then start planning your first investment.

Set realistic goals according to the size of your bankroll. (Bankroll is the amount of ready cash you have available for investment purposes only.) The first investment you make will require approximately $4,500, of which $3,000 will be a down payment and $1,500 will be used for fix-up funds. This is all the money you will ever need. All further investments will be paid for out of income generated from the first property purchased. Of course, if you're fortunate enough to possess enough ready cash to make additional investments, then you can advance at a faster pace. Otherwise, you will need to wait approximately one year for the first property to generate enough cash for you to invest in a second property.

Thus, after one year you will own two properties. It will take only 8 months to accumulate enough earnings to buy a third property. Since you own three properties after 20 months' time, you can purchase a fourth property with accumulated earnings from the other three within another 6 months. Total elapsed time from Day 1 is now 26 months, and you now own four properties. Realistically, you could now purchase a new property every 6 months for the next 3 years using accumulated earnings from the properties you already own.

Therefore, set a goal of purchasing your first fixer-upper using $4,500 within the next 6 months. If you don't have

$4,500 in cash, then set your first goal to save it, and make your second goal to buy a fixer-upper with your savings.

Based on this timetable and starting with an initial bankroll of $4,500, within 5 years and 2 months you will have accumulated 10 income-producing properties. This would be an ideal goal, because the astounding result would be $30,000 per year additional net income and over $275,000 in accumulated equity. Not bad for a $4,500 investment made 5 years and 2 months ago!

THE OVERALL PLAN IN A NUTSHELL

Make a good buy; fix it up, making the sales price, the financing, and the entire house appealing; then sell it outright or on installment for a handsome profit that pays you monthly dividends for the next 20 years. These monthly dividends are reinvested into a second property as you continue to fix up and sell, reinvest, fix up and sell. This is of course an oversimplification, but it's true. If you make a good buy, do a nice job fixing it up (keeping the decorating and overall refurbishment in good taste, i.e., mild earth-tones), price the property right, (keeping the financing profitable for you, yet still reasonable to the buyer), there is no doubt you will profit from investing in fixer-uppers.

A good buy not only means you bought at a good price, but that you purchased a property with architectural appeal (well-designed with a few improvements that will appeal to the majority of potential buyers). A good buy will also have low-interest-rate assumable financing, which will allow you, in turn, to offer reasonable financing to your buyer.

The best method to use after you buy and fix up property is the lease-option. This method of selling on installment offers you tremendous profit and growth, while at the same time avoids all the pitfalls of conventional methods of leasing and selling. The lease-option concept is explained in Chapter 7.

This book is dedicated to the millions of Americans who thirst for financial freedom. Good luck.

1

How to Finance a Fixer-Upper

To succeed at real estate investment, look at borrowing money as a way of accumulating surplus income. In other words, the debt you incur on a particular property is not really a debt you will pay back with your hard-earned money, but actually a debt that will generate income that will pay back that debt plus provide surplus income. You are actually becoming partners with the lender (except you don't share the profits), which will enable you to finance a property that you will rent out, paying back the debt with the tenant's money and earning yourself a profit.

So don't be apprehensive about incurring debt that's associated with income-producing property. As long as each property purchased develops more income than it costs to operate, all debt will be manageable.

METHODS OF FINANCE

Loan Assumption

Assumption of existing low-interest loans is the most inexpensive, easiest, and most profitable way to finance real estate. The best loans to assume are existing VA and FHA loans. These are loans that previous owners originated and are fully assumable by anyone without qualification whatsoever. That's right: no credit report, no points, no questions, and only a very small assumption fee.

Not only are VA and FHA loans the most attractive from a buyer's point of view, but when you sell, your buyer can assume the same VA and FHA loans.

Do not mistake assuming existing VA and FHA loans with obtaining new VA and FHA loans. The difference is that existing VA/FHA loans were originated by past owners and are now fully assumable by anyone. To create a new VA/FHA loan requires credit qualification and an appraisal, much like obtaining conventional financing. New VA/FHA loans are discussed later in this chapter.

Conventional Financing

Most new first loans on real estate are made by savings and loan associations. Suppose you found a home with no existing assumable financing, or the owner owned it free and clear and wanted all his cash out of it. Then the only way to finance it would be to find a conventional lender to lend you the money.

Under conventional lending through your local savings and loan, the following would be the procedure for acquiring a loan: You would meet with a loan officer, who would have you fill out a loan application. He would then take a copy of the offer you made on the property, tell you the going interest rate, and then tell you he will call you and let you know whether they will make the loan. The loan officer would then initiate a credit report on you and verify the employment and income you reported on the application. After that, he would order an appraisal on the subject property; once he had everything in order, he would call you and offer or refuse to make the loan. If everything went right, the loan officer usually would give you an answer within three weeks of your request.

With conventional financing, the lender usually requires at least 20 percent down payment. Sometimes lenders will go as low as 10 percent, but will require you to pay for private mortgage insurance (PMI), which costs 0.25 percent interest. The purpose of the PMI is to protect the lender for the additional 10 percent loaned, in case of default.

Some conventional loans can be assumed without qualification. However, this is extremely rare because most conventional loans have acceleration clauses, which keep them from being assumed. Acceleration, or due-on-sale, clauses give the lender the right to call all monies owed due and payable upon the happening of a certain stated event, such as a sale.

VA Loans

VA loans are government-backed loans extended to veterans, entitling them to borrow up to 100 percent for homes, mobile homes, and farms. The VA loan is underwritten and processed by conventional lenders, but a portion is guaranteed by the Veterans Administration against default by the borrower. Since VA loan rates are usually below market interest rates, the VA allows the underwriting lender to charge points to make up the difference between the yield of a VA loan and that of a conventional loan. One point is the equivalent of 1 percent of the loan. If the lender charged 1 point for a $50,000 loan, the amount would be $500. Points for a VA loan are usually paid by the seller.

To protect the veteran and assist the lender in approving the loan, the Veterans Administration will have the property appraised and will issue a Certificate of Reasonable Value (CRV). A veteran may purchase a home at any price, but a VA loan cannot be secured for more than the CRV. For any amount in excess of the CRV, the veteran must pay cash.

FHA Loans

FHA loans are government-backed loans, made under the

supervision of the Federal Housing Administration (FHA). They are available to anyone who meets the FHA's requirements. An FHA loan is underwritten and processed by conventional lending institutions, and the FHA insures the lender against default. Thus, the lender is able to grant longer and more lenient terms. FHA loans offer below-market interest rates and a smaller down payment than conventional financing. And, as with VA loans, FHA loans involve points to boost the yield to the underwriting lender.

Land Contract (Contract of Sale)

A land contract, or contract of sale, is strictly a contract between buyer and seller, without the involvement of a financial intermediary. The buyer agrees to purchase a property and pays principal and interest to the seller along with a down payment. The title to the property remains with the seller until the conditions of the contract are fulfilled. The buyer retains possession of the property. Should the buyer default on the agreement, the property reverts to the seller.

This type of financing is ideal during "tight money" conditions, as interest rates on a land contract can be negotiated between buyer and seller, often at lesser rates than current market interest rates. In addition, existing low-interest-rate financing can be left intact while a new land contract can be written at a higher rate of interest, thus "wrapping" the existing financing.

For example, if your property has low-interest-rate financing that you wish to keep intact, you can sell it on contract. The contract could stipulate that the buyer pays a higher fixed rate of interest and you continue to pay on the existing low-interest-rate loans, thus wrapping the existing loans with a new loan agreement. You would make a profit on the spread in interest rates. This might compensate you for not having the use of the entire sales price at the time you sell the property.

Purchase-Money Seconds

Purchase-money second mortgages are creative financing at its best. A purchase-money second loan is created when the seller is willing to carry back a second loan for the equity in the property, instead of taking cash. For example, you buy a house for $70,000 with a down payment of $3,000, and you assume the existing $50,000 loan. The $17,000 balance remaining is carried by the seller in the form of a second mortgage payable at $170 per month at 9 percent for 10 years. In this example, $20,000 represents the owner's equity in the property. You pay $3,000 down, and instead of $17,000 cash, the owner takes back a second mortgage of $17,000.

Two years ago I found a great property that, at first glance, appeared impossible to purchase with a small down payment. It had an existing 8 percent first loan of $40,000, and the seller wanted $25,000 down. The list price was $119,000, and the agent doubted that the seller would be willing to carry back a second loan. I made an offer of $92,000; I would pay $10,000 down and assume the existing first loan of $40,000, and the seller was to carry back a second loan at 9 percent for the balance of $42,000. Neither my agent nor the seller's agent thought this offer had a one-in-a-hundred chance of being accepted, but to everyone's surprise the seller made a counter offer at a price of $96,000, and I accepted. The only changes from my original offer were the price and the amount the seller would carry back, which increased $4,000 to $46,000 at 9 percent.

In essence, I created $46,000 in new low-interest-rate financing on a property that first appeared would never sell under such lucrative terms. Six months after we purchased this money-maker, we had it sold for $115,000 at 11.5 percent and would clear $350 per month on it for the next 20 years.

Based on this experience, you never really know whether a seller will carry back a note unless you at least attempt to create secondary financing by making a legitimate offer.

Sellers tend to change their demands when their property has been sitting on the market for an extended length of time.

Take-Out Seconds

A take-out second loan is created when the owner of a property takes out a loan against his or her equity in the property. Typically a take-out second would be made for home improvements, to finance a college education, to buy more property, etc. Here a financial institution or investor would make the second loan, which would be secured by a second mortgage recorded against the subject property.

In most cases a second loan could be taken out for 80 percent of the equity in the property. Take-out seconds are probably the most expensive type of loan you can incur. In today's market, second loans are in the range of 15 percent with origination fees of 1 or 2 points. I would recommend taking out a second loan only when you can use the proceeds from the loan to purchase additional property, and only when that property is an excellent bargain because income from the investment can cover the cost of the new take-out loan.

All-Inclusive Mortgage

The all-inclusive (wraparound) loan is one of the best creative financing methods used today. It enables the seller to maintain the existing low-interest financing while a new all-inclusive loan wraps around the existing loans. The seller keeps making payments on the existing loans while the buyer makes payments to the seller on the new all-inclusive loan.

A wraparound loan is most useful when the seller wishes to keep intact valuable existing low-interest-rate financing. Here's how it works. You are asking $89,000 for a property with two existing low-interest-rate loans. To keep these valuable loans intact, you create and carry a new wraparound loan at a higher interest rate, which enables you to make a profit on the difference in interest rates.

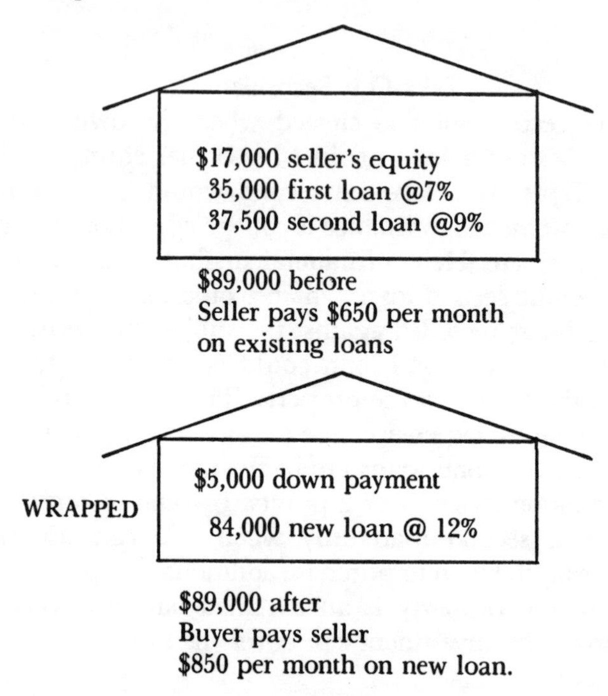

In the example, the seller creates and carries a new loan for $84,000 at 12 percent, which equals $850 per month. The seller continues to pay on original first and second loans equaling $650 per month and has a profit of $200 per month.

Using First and Second Notes as Cash

In purchasing a property, first and second notes can be used as the equivalent of cash. Notes you own (money owed to you) accompanied by cash or other consideration will actually make the total down payment more attractive. As an example, you could offer a down payment of $20,000 to be in the form of $10,000 in cash and $10,000 in a second note. (I once used a 1977 Dodge Van and a second note to purchase a property.)

Using notes as a down payment has a big advantage for you, the buyer. If you had to convert the note to cash (sell it to an investor), you could expect the note to be discounted 20 to 25 percent. In other words, if you owned a note for $10,000 and you converted it to cash, you might receive $7,500, which is $10,000 less a 25 percent discount.

The actual amount of discount will primarily depend on payment history of the note, interest rate, remaining years to payoff, payment amount, and equity in the property.

REFINANCING VERSUS A SECOND LOAN

If you have owned a home for a number of years and have a large equity position in the property, you might want to pull some of that equity out of the property and turn it into cash for additional investments. You will have to decide whether to refinance (paying off the old loan with a new loan) or take out a second loan and keep the first loan intact.

For borrowing to be profitable, you must use the borrowed money to bring a greater return than the cost of the loan. Remember, money borrowed is a debt and must be repaid with interest.

Refinancing

If you can refinance with an interest rate that is at least 2 points below the interest rate of the loan you are replacing, then by all means refinance. But in most cases, especially when the home has had a single owner for the last 10 years or more, the existing mortgage will likely be at an interest rate far below the current market interest rate. If this holds true, then it would be unwise to refinance because that would eliminate the value of the existing low-interest loan by replacing it with a costlier high-interest loan.

Take for example a home purchased five years ago for $50,000 with a $40,000 first mortgage at 8 percent interest for a term of 30 years. The principal and interest payment was $300 per month. The remaining principal balance owing after five years of payments was $38,000. Today's market value of the home is $80,000. Therefore, there is $42,000 equity in the home ($80,000 – $38,000 = $42,000).

If the home is refinanced at an 11.5 percent rate of interest, the lender would advance a maximum of 80 percent of the market value, of which $38,000 must be applied toward paying off the balance on the original loan. Thus, there would be $26,000 in net proceeds ($80,000 × 80% = $64,000; $64,000 – $38,000 = $26,000). The new first mortgage would require monthly payments of $634 to amortize principal and interest over the term of 30 years. (*Amortize* means to pay off debt in equal payments.)

If a second mortgage is arranged for an amount equal to that of refinancing, which is $26,000, the lender would normally charge about two percentage points more for a maximum term of 15 years. Therefore, on a loan of $26,000 for 15 years at 13.5 percent, the monthly payment would be $338. Total monthly payments for the next 15 years including the existing payment on the first mortgage would be $638 ($338 + $300). After 15 years the second mortgage would be paid in full, leaving only the $300 monthly payment on the first mortgage. (See the following examples for a complete comparison.)

Refinancing

Amount of net proceeds: $26,000
Payment on first loan: $634
Term of loan: 30 years
Total amount paid over term of loan: $228,240

Taking Out a Second Mortgage

Amount of net proceeds: $26,000
Payment on first loan: $300
Term remaining on first loan: 25 years
Payment on second loan: $338
Term remaining on second loan: 15 years
Total paid over term of loans: $150,840

Over the full term of the loan, taking out a second mortgage as opposed to refinancing saved $77,400. There are two basic reasons for the difference. First, refinancing the property at the higher rate of 11.5 percent adds 3.5 percentage points to a 30-year loan, of which over half the proceeds went to pay off $38,000 on the original principal amount. The second reason is that although 13.5 percent interest on a second mortgage appears, at first glance, to be excessive, it is only for a term of 15 years.

During the life of an amortized loan, the initial payments are mostly interest. As time goes on, the interest paid becomes a smaller portion of the payment, and more of the payment goes toward principal payoff (equity buildup).

The only time to prefer refinancing a home over taking out a second mortgage would be when prevailing market interest rates for first mortgages are below the rate on the existing first mortgage. Usually the difference should be at least two points.

EQUITY SHARING

Equity sharing is also known as shared equity, equity participation, equity partnership, and shared appreciation. It stems from the concept of pairing cash-short buyers with cash-rich investors. The two share ownership of the property, and both will gain when it is later sold for a profit.

Here's how it works. Let's say you are short of cash and your parents wish to help you invest in a home. Your parents agree to make the down payment in exchange for a one-half interest in the house. You agree to occupy the house, maintain it, and pay fair market rent to your parents for their interest in the property. You and your parents split the costs of principal and interest, property taxes, and insurance. Your half-owner parents, because they are rental property investors, can claim income tax deductions of mortgage interest, property taxes, and depreciation. Your tax deductions will be the same as for all homeowners—mortgage interest and property taxes.

Equity sharing is advantageous because it eliminates cumbersome loans between co-owners. Furthermore, it eliminates income taxes levied on interest paid to the co-owner/lender. If, in contrast, your parents had made the down payment in the form of a generous and helpful gift, they would receive no tax advantage.

Taking title to a home under equity sharing is the same as purchasing one on your own. Both parties go on the title according to the laws of the state where the property is located. Also, both parties sign the mortgage note and take responsibility for its payment.

An equity sharing transaction requires one additional step to home ownership. A contract between the co-owners is necessary to spell out exactly important points of the agreement, such as ownership percentages, rent to be charged, buyout options, specifics on resale, and responsibility for repairs and maintenance. The contract should also specify procedures in the event of death, default, disability, bankruptcy of a co-owner, or acts of God (such as floods and tornadoes).

Therefore, equity sharing can be advantageous to both the investor and the owner/occupant. The owner/occupant can eventually buy out the investor, sell the house, and use the proceeds for a down payment on another home. The investor has many tax advantages from the ownership interest and can share in the home's appreciation.

LOOK OUT FOR PROBLEMS

Before I can present you with sound financing concepts, you must understand the problems faced by the inexperienced real estate investor. Two major problems are loss of control and the cumbersome events that occur when dealing with third parties—the bank and federal agencies.

Loss of Control

During the initial years of my investment career, I had bought and sold several houses. Even though each property was unique, with its own problems and solutions, I managed to turn a profit on each one. As time went on and I became more experienced, something changed my plans drastically: I developed "seller's remorse" and began losing control of profitability due to cumbersome events.

Seller's remorse is the regret I felt when I sold my investments. After combing the city for a good investment—which was done in my spare time since I had a full-time job, making several offers and finally having one accepted, fixing up the property and selling it, I always went through this condition of seller's remorse. Sure I made a tidy profit, but income taxes on profits seriously eroded the overall profitability. Once I had received the proceeds, they would lie dormant until I could find another house to invest in. The question confronted me: How could I sell the property, minimize my tax liability, and still maintain control of the property?

Third-Party Financing

A third party can be a conventional lender or the VA or FHA. What happened to me on several occasions involving third parties has probably occurred to many home sellers.

One morning I answered the phone. "Mr. McLean, I have an offer on your house, and I would like to come over and present it to you." When the Realtor arrived with the offer I was pleasantly surprised to see that the earnest money agreement matched my full asking price. He said there shouldn't be any problem having the buyer qualify under the VA loan requirements.

This was unbelievable, I thought, a full price offer. What was to take place over the next five months became an all-too-believable nightmare.

Before the Realtor left he said, "Keep in mind that the buyer has to qualify, and it may take a little longer because the buyer is still awaiting his eligibility papers." When he walked out the door I began reminiscing about what life was like in the army—a life of "hurry up and wait." Instead of three weeks to qualify, it took five because the buyer's tip income was difficult to substantiate, but he finally qualified. Next came the VA appraiser. For some unknown reason, he was on time.

Then there was the VA inspection. (I was beginning to believe there was no end in sight to this cumbersome bureaucracy.) But why should I worry about an inspection . . . I just spent a month's time and $2,500 hard-earned dollars getting this house in good shape to sell. Four days after the VA inspector left, I received his report in the mail. Good grief, it was three pages long and read like he had just inspected and failed a downtown slum run on charity. I had to correct all these shortcomings before the VA would approve the loan. I figured an additional $1,000 and a month's time to correct these shortcomings. One month and another payment later, the VA inspector came by and made his final approval.

Now I thought we were getting somewhere. The buyers were anxious to move in; I was anxious to be cashed out; everybody was anxious to close the deal—except the bank!

I'm sure most of you have heard of points. Those are extra fees banks charge to originate loans. They're like federal excise taxes or surcharges utility companies charge when they need to make more money from us consumers. In a VA transaction the seller pays the points, and at the time I accepted the offer the points were 2. But now, since almost four months had expired since the offer was accepted, the points had grown to 5. In other words, in the beginning I had to pay 2 points (2 percent of a $60,000 loan, or $1,200), now I had to pay 5 points, or $3,000, or an additional $1,800 because of cumbersome third-party events.

These additional costs were presented to me at the escrow office on the day of closing. I could have refused to pay them, thus canceling out my sale. However, I'm sure the buyers would have sued for performance, and I envisioned a long court battle should that occur. So I begrudgingly signed the papers, took my $1,800 loss in points, and swore that I'd never get involved in a situation like that again.

This transaction had been such a time-consuming nightmare that I started asking myself how I could accomplish the same goals without third-party intervention to entangle my transaction. I was determined to create a method to control my cash flow.

There is a time and place for VA/FHA financing, in spite of their cumbersome ways. They do offer a low interest rate with low down payment financing, and help to stabilize the real estate lending market by guaranteeing these loans.

Compliance with VA/FHA regulations and the ensuing time delays create several problems if you are the seller; however, their cumbersome regulations and delays do benefit the buyer. For the small investor, the greatest benefit is that existing VA/FHA loans are fully assumable, without qualification. That means a lot when you can assume loans that are far below prevailing market interest rates. In fact, these low-interest assumable loans will be the key to solving the investment problems described in this section.

The Remedy: Loan Assumption and Installment Sales

The hassles of dealing with overburdened federal agencies and conventional lenders made me think—there had to be a better way. The answer, in simple terms, was to *assume existing low-interest loans and sell on installment.* Sounds easy, doesn't it? Well it is—and my portfolio of properties is living proof to this approach to investing.

Let's look at some examples of property bought and sold using loan assumption and installment sale versus originating a new loan and conventional sale (see page 24).

Note the difference in monthly payments—you save $111 per month by assuming. In total closing costs, you save $725. Note also the time to close; you save plenty of time, and time is money. (See page 25.)

As you can see, assuming existing loans saves you time and money. By selling on installment you also save the points, and in many cases a healthy sales commission.

Comparison on Acquisition

Assumption

Purchase price	$60,000
Down payment	4,000
Assume loan @ 7%	30,000
Seller carries second loan @ 9%	26,000
Payments on first and second loans	467
Assumption fee	$ 35
Total cost	$ 35
Closing time	14 days

Originating New Loan

Purchase price	$60,000
Down payment	4,000
New loan @ 11%	56,000
No second loan	0
Payments on first loan	578
Loan origination fee	$ 560
Credit report	75
Appraisal fee	125
Total cost	$ 760
Closing time	60–180 days

Structuring the Second Loan

When you purchase, you have to be sure that the purchase-money second you created has no acceleration clause. If no acceleration clause is included, then it can be assumed. If there were an acceleration clause (most conventional lenders put these in their loan documents), then the loan you created technically could not be assumed by another buyer without the note holder demanding the balance due when you sell.

Comparison on Sale

Installment Sale

Sales price	$66,000
Down payment	2,000
Points	0
Sales commission	0
Inspection	0

FHA/VA Sale

Sales price	$66,000
Down payment	2,000
Seller pays points (4 pts.)	2,560
Sales commission (6%)	3,960
Inspection (approx.)	500

Another important point is that you can write the second loan a number of ways. If you want the payment to be low, then specify that interest only is payable, with a balloon payment of principal at the end of the term. If you amortize the entire loan over the full term, you won't have a balloon payment, but your cash flow will be reduced substantially from the higher loan payment. For example, a $17,500 second loan at 10 percent interest only is payable in monthly installments of $146. A $17,500 second loan at 10 percent fully amortized for 10 years is payable in monthly installments of $231.

Chapter 7 shows you exactly how to sell your investments on installment and why it is the most profitable method and the easiest to accomplish. The lease-option method is the investment concept I use to avoid third-party entanglements and to get the most for my money.

PITFALLS TO AVOID

In the last few years institutional lenders have created new forms of financing to protect themselves from what they consider a hazard to business: fluctuating interest rates. These new loans include adjustable-rate mortgages

(ARMs), graduated payment mortgages (GPMs), negative amortization loans, and any other kind of financing that allows the lender to charge more during the term of the loan when market interest rates are on the rise.

Adjustable-rate mortgages allow the lender to increase or decrease the interest rate charged for the loan based on a predetermined government index. The increase or decrease is usually limited to 5 percentage points. Note that the rate is as likely to increase as decrease.

Graduated payment mortgages are designed to gradually increase in amount of payment over the term of the loan. This form of financing presumes the borrower will steadily make more money and thus be able to afford the increase in monthly payment.

Negative amortization loans are the exact opposite of a typical amortized loan. In a typical amortized loan, principal and interest are paid, leaving a smaller principal amount owed after payment. Under a negative amortization loan, the amount owed *increases* after each payment. That's an interesting feeling . . . paying on a loan, then after a few months realizing that you now owe more than when you started making payments.

These forms of financing are definitely hazardous to your business because you have no control over the costs of your loans. Avoid them by all means. Stick with fixed-rate financing and assumption of low-interest-rate loans. Remember, avoid costly entanglements and dirty surprises from lenders who can ask for more money during the term of a loan because you agreed to an adjustable-rate mortgage.

POINTS TO REMEMBER

Generally, the easiest and most economical way to finance your future real estate investments is through loan assumption and having the seller carry back a note for his equity in the property. Keep in mind that the lower the interest rate you assume, the more profitable your investment will be. Assumable loans will give you built-in financing on the property, which is very valuable when it comes time to resell.

If you decide to use conventional financing, be prepared to meet the costs of originating the loan. Remember, too, that conventional loans are seldom assumable, which seriously inhibits the resalability of the property. Conventional financing would be recommended, and only at a reasonable fixed rate of interest (10 percent or less), only when you can make such a good buy that you could make a great enough profit from resale to offset the high costs and inflexibility of such a loan.

New FHA financing is recommended only when interest rates are low. FHA requires that you pay at least 4 percent of the purchase price as a down payment and that you intend to live on the property. Again, be wary of extended escrows and cumbersome events.

In conclusion, try to keep your financing simple by avoiding cumbersome third-party lenders. Always try to assume existing low-interest-rate financing. Furthermore, try to create low-interest-rate financing by having the seller carry back a note for as long a term as possible and without a due-on-sale clause. Then you will have built-in financing allowing you plenty of flexibility when it comes time to resell.

2

Buy Right to Sell Right

This chapter attempts to supply the information you'll need to purchase a house that will offer you a steady positive cash flow over the next 10 to 20 years and shelter a portion of your income from income taxes.

SINGLE-FAMILY RESIDENCES: THE WISEST CHOICE

There are two types of investors, big and small. The big investor has usually gotten big by making small investments, accumulating wealth, and turning to bigger and better things—like huge apartment buildings and shopping centers. The small investor is the rest of us—the ones who need more income, more tax shelter, more accumulated wealth, and the eventual achievement of the milestone of being a big investor.

For the small investor, specializing in single-family residences (SFRs) is the wisest choice. There is a plentiful supply of SFRs with much demand. There are plenty of small investors and first-time home buyers who create this demand. For a typical middle-income family, home ownership is definitely their number one priority.

But why specialize at all? A medical doctor specializes in one particular field of medicine and an attorney specializes in one particular field of law to become an expert in that particular field. It's much more practical, and probably easier, to be an expert in one particular field than to become a jack-of-all-trades, master of none.

If you stick to learning about SFRs, values in the surrounding neighborhood, and typical selling prices and costs per square foot of homes throughout the city, then you can succeed as a real estate investor. That's because, essentially, all you really need to know is what's a good buy, then how to fix it up and what it will sell for.

INGREDIENTS OF A GOOD BUY

The ingredients of a good buy form the foundation of a solid investment that will pay dividends for years to come. These ingredients are:

1. Buy at a good price.
2. Buy only fixer-uppers, in which you can create "sweat equity."
3. Assume low-interest loans.
4. Buy with as little down as possible.
5. Avoid short-term balloon payments, prepayment penalties, and acceleration clauses.
6. Find motivated sellers.

Buy at a Good Price

Probably your top priority is to buy the home at a good price. Remember, your intention is to make a profit and develop a steady positive cash flow. If the price is too high, reconsider the purchase, even if all the other ingredients are there. You don't have to buy everything in sight. Be patient—keep looking; the good buys are out there. You just have to keep looking, and you'll find them.

Buy Only Fixer-Uppers

What exactly is a fixer-upper, and exactly what are you supposed to look for?

Fixer-uppers come in all shapes, sizes, and degree of work needed to refurbish the entire property. Ideally, a good prospect in a fixer-upper is a single-family home that just needs some cleaning up and a cosmetic paint job inside and out. Next in priority would be a similar home that needs cleaning up and paint, but also a new carpet, some kitchen tile, and a new bathroom sink. This home would be less in priority only because it will cost more to fix up than the other home.

The rule of thumb for evaluating whether a property is worth fixing up is that every dollar invested in fixing up should yield at least two dollars in increased property value. In other words, can you clean up the property and paint it inside and out for $1,000, and then sell the property for at least $2,000 more than you paid for it?

The degree of work needed doesn't matter; you can profit as long as the value of the improvements is twice what those improvements cost. Of course, another consideration is that if you have a limited bankroll to finance improvements, you are limited in the amount you can spend on fixing it up. If this is the case, then just stick to buying fixer-uppers that need only small amounts of capital to fix them up.

Properties become run-down due to lack of proper maintenance. It takes money and hard work to get them back into good condition. In a lot of cases the owner has owned the property a while, experienced being a landlord and didn't like it, and for whatever reason doesn't want to put more money in the now-vacant property.

Usually many of these problems look a lot worse than they really are. The landscaping is overgrown, and trash is strewn about the front yard. The interior probably looks like a gang of gorillas stayed too long and left their banana peels strewn about the floor. Windows are broken, the place needs a new carpet, and it stinks to high heaven. This unappealing condition is not uncommon. People leave homes in this shabby condition all the time. The point is, all that filth and destruction lowers prices. All you have to do is determine what it will cost to clean and fix it up, and the price for which you can reasonably sell it.

Assume Low-Interest Loans

Remember, third-party entanglements just cost you hard-earned money and wasted time. You maintain control and save time and money by assuming low-interest-rate loans. Furthermore, it is necessary to acquire low-interest assumable loans to sell on installment to your buyers. Low-interest loans are considered to be anything below 10 percent. Avoid loans at 10 percent or higher.

Let's compare the cost of a $50,000 loan at 7 percent for 20 years with a $50,000 loan at 11 percent for 20 years. At 7 percent the monthly payment is $387.65, and at 11 percent the monthly payment is $516.10. The difference is $128.45 per month. Over the full term of the loan, the difference would be $30,828 (20 years × 12 months × $128.45). In other words, if one couple had a $50,000 loan on their house and were paying 11 percent, while their neighbors had the same loan, but instead paid 7 percent interest, over the full term of the loan (20 years) the couple who paid 11 percent interest would have paid $30,828 more for their home than their neighbors.

$50,000 loan for
20 years @ 7% = $387.65
per month; over 20 years
total payout would be $93,036.

Differential is
$30,828

$50,000 loan for
20 years @ 11% = $516.10
per month; over 20 years
total payout would be $123,864

These interest rate differentials are important. The lower the interest rate on the property you buy, the more money you will make when you eventually sell on installment at a higher rate of interest.

Besides these substantial savings under an assumption during the term of the loan, the costs of creating a new conventional loan can be staggering. Typically, the lender will charge anywhere from 2 to 8 points to originate the loan. On a $50,000 loan that would be $1,000 to $4,000 in point fees. Other costs are an appraisal fee of $150 and $75 for a credit report. All these additional costs seriously erode your profitability. These extraordinary costs can be completely eliminated through a simple loan assumption.

Buy with as Little Down as Possible

Minimizing your down payment cannot be emphasized enough. Investing too much money in a down payment reduces your return on investment and seriously limits your selling options. Excessive down payments require you to recover large amounts of cash through a sale, which seriously limits the number of prospective buyers who might be interested in your property.

For example, let's say you have $18,000 in ready cash available for investment. You could put the entire amount into one property, or you could buy four properties with this significant amount. Investing the entire amount in one property would limit your future purchasing power because you have nothing left over for further investment. Your return on investment would be smaller than it would be with a smaller down payment. Furthermore, you would tend to require more of a down payment from a buyer in order to recoup your huge investment, thus inhibiting the property's salability. Besides, the net income and return on investment would be much greater if you used $18,000 to buy four properties instead of one.

LEVERAGE

Purchasing something of value (a home) using something

of much lesser value (down payment) is using leverage. The smaller the down payment, the more leverage you are using; the larger the down payment, the less the leverage.

RETURN ON INVESTMENT

The lower the leverage, the lower the rate of return on investment. For example, assume you bought a home for $50,000 cash, held it for a year, and then sold it for $55,000. In this particular transaction you would have a profit of $5,000 from a $50,000 investment, or a 10 percent return on investment ($5,000 divided by $50,000). Now suppose you bought a similar property for $50,000, but in this case you put $2,000 down and financed the balance. A year later you sold for $55,000, earning a $5,000 profit. On this transaction you received a $5,000 profit based on a $2,000 down payment, which is a 250 percent return on investment ($5,000 divided by $2,000). If we take this example even further and use a down payment of only $1,000, the return on investment would be 500 percent ($5,000 divided by $1,000). As you can see, the less you put down on a property, the more leverage you are using and the more return on investment you'll receive.

Avoid Short-Term Balloon Payments, Prepayment Penalties, and Acceleration Clauses

Balloon payments are payments due at the end of a loan obligation. They essentially are a promise to pay additional cash at some future time. If the promise isn't kept, it most certainly will cause a foreclosure. Long-term (five years or more) balloon obligations are much easier to live with because you have plenty of time to prepare for the payoff. If you're going to structure secondary financing you are obligated to pay, try to extend the term of the balloon obligation as far into the future as possible. Then you'll have more protection and time to prepare for its eventual payoff.

Prepayment penalties and acceleration clauses are clauses banks use to entangle the sale of real estate. These items may not seem bad at the time of purchase, but at the time of sale they could ruin the whole transaction.

Find the Best Buys: From Motivated Sellers

Motivated sellers are those who, due to circumstances, are more prepared to sell below market value than an unmotivated seller. Circumstances that motivate sellers are divorce, death in the family, job relocation, vacant rental, and a property that has been on the market for an extended period. In certain cases you might have a combination of these circumstances, where a property is vacant and has been on the market for an extended period. In a case like that, where the owner is still making payments with nothing coming in, he will be extremely motivated and ready to look at any offer.

A FINAL TIP

In conclusion, I would like to offer one more tip on buying right to sell right. Lower-valued homes, those that are affordable to lower-income and middle-income families, are in much more demand as rentals and resales than are high-priced homes. This is simply because more people can afford a lower-priced home. Therefore, especially in the early stages of your investment experience, try to stick with buying and selling the more affordable homes in your area. That way, the higher demand will make your rentals and resales easier to rent or sell.

BUY RIGHT TO SELL RIGHT REVIEW CHECKLIST

1. Specialize in single-family residences.
2. Buy at a good price.
3. Buy only fix-up properties whereby you can create value.
4. Assume low-interest loans where you can resell at a higher rate of interest.
5. Buy with as little down as possible using maximum leverage creating a high rate of return on investment.

6. Avoid short-term balloon payments and acceleration clauses which can inhibit the salability of your property.
7. And remember, the best buys come from motivated sellers.

3

Where to Find Your Diamond in the Rough

REALTOR AND MLS

When you're looking for a property, a good real estate agent is your number one priority and a great asset to have for a number of reasons. A good agent is looking out for your interest. To work effectively, he should know exactly what you're looking for. Tell the agent you want a fixer-upper single-family residence with low-interest assumable loans and a small down payment. Tell him why this is what you're looking for in a property and what you plan to do with it. A good agent has access to a multiple-listing service (MLS) that covers every home listed for sale with a broker in your area. It's the agent's job to keep abreast of what's available and to be looking for property you might be interested in. Furthermore, the agent is important to you because as an agent, he has a key to a lock box that opens the door to any property listed in the MLS.

With regard to MLS listings, bear in mind that output from a computer is only as good as the information entered into it. Many times you will find that a property listed in the MLS computer is not up to date, which could cost you time and energy. Get in the habit of calling for an update on the property before you take the time and gasoline needed to inspect it. Often you'll find that the particular property you're interested in has already been sold, or that it's been taken off the market for some reason.

Finally, a good agent can be helpful to you when you're dealing with for-sale-by-owners. In this particular case no commission would be involved, since the home is not listed with a broker. But your agent can be helpful during negotiations, assisting you as a third-party arbitrator looking out for your best interest. Since he would receive no commission, a nominal fee would be appropriate for the time and services rendered.

NEWSPAPERS

You'll find many homes for sale listed in the classified section of your local newspaper. Circle the properties that appear interesting, then start calling about them. Inquire into the financing available and the down payment requirements. Get as much information as you can. Then, if the property sounds promising, make an appointment with the owner to visit the property.

FORECLOSURES

Some of the best buys I ever made came from distress sales. It is possible to invest in property at any of the stages of foreclosure, and foreclosure property has always been an extremely popular form of investment, because such property is usually sold at prices that are often far below fair market value.

Foreclosure real estate is a specialized market. The availability of such property tends to vary substantially with the overall economy. For example, during the late 1960s, when the inflation rate was slower than it is now, banks and savings and loan institutions had large inventories of foreclosure property on their books, especially in declining neighborhoods. A higher rate of inflation means faster equity buildup as values increase, so that in periods of runaway inflation less distressed property is available, since the owners can more often meet their obligations through refinancing.

The Three Stages of Foreclosure

Foreclosure takes place in up to three stages. First, a property owner who defaults on a loan is notified by the bank or lending institution that it is initiating legal procedures that will lead to a foreclosure sale. Second, unless the payments in arrears are made, plus penalties and costs, the property goes up for sale at public auction. The highest bidder pays off the loan (in cash) and claims the property. Finally, if the property does not sell at auction, it reverts to the lending institution, and is then called REO (Real Estate Owned) property.

Acquiring real estate during the first stage of foreclosure can often lead to some spectacular investments. However, the trials and difficulties associated with such property are often equally spectacular, and in all the wrong ways. Associated with foreclosure property are often all sorts of hidden problems in the form of liens against the property. While you may be able to buy the property away from the owner quite easily, you may then find that you must also buy it back from the IRS, county tax assessor, or some other entity.

Unless you do exhaustive research before getting involved in a foreclosure property, you can get stuck having your cash tied up for months waiting for liens against the property to be cleared up, or for title searches to be conducted. In the end, your "bargain" may cost a lot more than you bargained for.

If a property has problems, you assume them when you purchase it. When you buy property in the first stage of foreclosure, you must do a lot of research and legwork, and even then you may end up with your funds tied up in escrow for long periods of time.

When you purchase a property in the second stage of foreclosure, at public auction, the same problem comes up—you must thoroughly investigate before you bid. In addition, you must pay cash for the property.

It is at the third stage that foreclosure property starts to become an extremely attractive venture. And before going any further, I'd like to share with you the bankers' philosophy toward foreclosure and REO property: they don't want anything to do with it!

Banks are in the business of lending money (and charging points). Of course, on a real estate loan, the property itself must be offered as collateral on the loan against the possibility of default by the buyer. But a bank's primary function is to take in deposits and loan out those deposits. Bankers are not happy about owning foreclosed real estate. They will work with a borrower, industriously at times, to avoid foreclosing. And they will make it very attractive to a purchaser to relieve them of the unwanted property once it's on the books as REO.

Acquiring Properties in the First Stage of Foreclosure

If you choose to work with distressed owners before a foreclosure sale, it is essential to your success that you follow these steps:

1. **Learn the Terminology.** It is important for you to learn foreclosure procedures and terminology so that you can portray yourself as a knowledgeable person to the property owners. This, in turn, will make it easier for you to function efficiently and effectively at acquiring worthwhile investments.

2. **Acquaint Yourself with the Sources.** You have four available resources to tap for property in distress: (a) Real Estate Owned, which is foreclosure property taken back by an institutional lender; (b) legal newspapers; (c) fee subscription services that publish defaults

and foreclosure sale notices; and (d) the county recorder's office, which records notices relevant to foreclosure.

3. **Choose a Territory in Which to Operate.** It is next to impossible to become an expert on real estate in distress for an entire state. Instead, concentrate your efforts in a specific small area where you can learn property values, and acquaint yourself with people who can be helpful in that area.
4. **Prepare a List of Potential Investments.** Now that you're acquainted with your territory and have tapped various sources of distressed property, you can begin to narrow your list down, through process of elimination, to properties that show a good profit potential.
5. **Prepare an Investment Analysis.** Once you have selected a number of properties that should be considered further, analyze what kind of offer you will make to the prospect.
6. **Meet and Negotiate with the Owner.** When you meet the owner, convey a mood of mutual assistance. Fully explain procedures to the distressed owner. Stress that only the specialist investor can truly remedy the distressed owner's precarious situation.
7. **Estimate the Costs.** When the troubled owner has revealed all the relevant facts about the property, you can estimate all the costs involved and prepare for the next step.
8. **Gather All the Data.** Now it's time to collect all the information and assess what you have. Are the loans in arrears, and if so how much, and are there liens against the property, etc?
9. **Closing the Deal.** During this phase you will be acquainted with the various forms necessary to close the deal and how to complete them inexpensively.

Let's examine these steps in greater detail.

LEARN THE TERMINOLOGY

What is foreclosure? It is the procedure where property pledged as security for a debt is sold to pay the debt in the event of default in payment and terms. The process varies from state to state, but the procedure is essentially similar throughout the country. The major difference in procedures is between states that use a mortgage as security on real property and those that use a deed of trust.

Mortgages and Deeds of Trust. *Mortgages* and *deeds of trust* (or trust deeds) are written instruments that create liens against real property. Should the borrower default on the loan (fail to make payments when due), mortgages and trust deeds will allow the lender to sell the property in order to satisfy the loan obligation.

In a mortgage, the two parties involved are referred to as the *mortgagor,* who is the property owner or borrower, and the *mortgagee,* or lender. A mortgage has two parts: the *mortgage note,* which is evidence of the debt, and the *mortgage contract,* which is security for the debt. The note promises to repay the loan, while the contract promises to convey title of the property to the mortgagee in case of default.

Should the mortgagor fail to make payments, the property can then be sold through foreclosure in a court action. In order to do so, the mortgagee must first obtain from the court a foreclosure judgment, which orders the sheriff to sell the property to the highest bidder (over and above what is due the lender). The property is then put up for public auction. Should a successful bid be made, the bidder receives from the sheriff a document known as the *certificate of sale.* In most cases, the bidder must then hold the certificate for one year, then receives a deed if the mortgagor does not pay the outstanding debt. In many states, if the mortgagor pays the outstanding debt during this period, he then retains ownership of the property, and the foreclosure sale is nullified. The mortgagor's privilege of redeeming the property is referred to as the mortgagor's *equity of redemption.*

Trust deeds are similar to mortgages except that an additional third party is involved and the foreclosure period is much shorter.

With a trust deed, the property owner-borrower is called the *trustor* and the lender is the *beneficiary.* The intermediate party, whose job it is to hold title to the property for the security of the lender, is called the *trustee.* Should the trustor default on the loan obligation, the subject property will be sold by the trustee at public auction through a "power of sale" clause contained in all trust deeds, without court procedure.

Foreclosure is initiated by a *notice of default,* which is recorded by the trustee, with a copy sent to the trustor. After three months, a *notice of sale* is posted on the property, and an advertisement for sale is carried in local newspapers once a week for three weeks. If during this period the trustor fails to pay the beneficiary sufficient funds to halt the foreclosure (overdue loan payments, plus interest, penalties and fees), the sale will be conducted by the trustee. Proceeds from foreclosure are disbursed to the beneficiary, then to any other lien holders.

In the United States, approximately half the states still use the traditional mortgage as security for real estate loans, while a few states use both the mortgage and a deed of trust as a security instrument. Lenders prefer the deed of trust because a foreclosure can be effected in one-third the time of a traditional mortgage and without court action.

This text refers only to mortgages. The reason for doing so is to simplify the text so it isn't necessary to discuss both instruments individually. Both the deed of trust and mortgage serve the same purpose; the only major difference is the method of enforcement in the case of default.

Assignment of Mortgage. A written financial document that transfers the rights of the beneficiary of a deed of trust to another party is called an *assignment* of a mortgage or deed of trust.

Substitution of Trustee. A written document, often located on the back of a deed of trust, that transfers trusteeship is a *substitution of trustee.* Transfers or substitutions of trustees are made for reasons such as convenience or more personal service. Legally the beneficiary can also be trustee. The purpose of doing so might be to gain control of a trustee sale.

Notice of Action (Lis Pendens). The legal term for a notice that a lawsuit is pending on the subject property is *lis pendens.* It gives notice that anyone acquiring an interest in the subject property after the date of notice may be bound by the outcome of the pending litigation.

Obviously, you should be very careful with such a notice attached to a property you're interested in. Unlike most other liens and attachments, a foreclosure sale seldom wipes out this pending litigation.

Recision. The act of nullifying the foreclosure process is called *recision.* It places the property back to its previous condition, before the default from the title records.

Power of Sale. The *power of sale* clause is written into all deeds of trust, giving the trustee the right to advertise and sell the secured property at public auction if the trustor defaults on the loan. This clause enables the trustee to sell the property without court order. When the sale is completed at the public auction, the trustee will convey title to the purchaser, use the funds from the proceeds to satisfy the beneficiary, then return surplus monies, if any, to the trustor. Once all this is accomplished, the trustor is entirely divested of the property and has no right of redemption.

ACQUAINT YOURSELF WITH THE SOURCES

Information regarding real estate in foreclosure is available through a variety of outlets. Services that provide such information vary throughout the country due to each state's legal requirements. Some states require the notice of default to be publicized in a legal newspaper. Many legal newspapers publish notices of default simply as a community service.

In addition to legal newspapers, some companies make available public record services on a fee subscription basis. Both legal newspapers and fee subscription services obtain their information directly from the county recorder's office. Their published information is rearranged into a more easily read form. The cost of this convenient service is substantially higher than that of legal newspapers or the free information available from the public records or the county recorder.

Of course, you could get information on recorded defaults directly from the county recorder. These data are recorded daily and are available for public use.

Once the default has been recorded and the redemption period has elapsed, the notice of sale is published. This legal notice cannot be found at the county recorder's office, because the trustee is required only to publish, not to record, this notice. You can obtain this information from subscription services, legal newspapers, and often in local newspapers that are authorized to publish these legal notices. Also, you'll often notice these postings on bulletin boards in your county courthouse.

Keep in mind that the services that publish notices of default are not liable for the accuracy of the information. You may find incorrect addresses or other data published by such services. The only data that can be deemed reliable are the actual recordings found in the county recorder's office.

These published services do not state whether the instrument in default is a first, second, or third mortgage. To determine which of the liens is in default, you'll have to make a personal visit to the county recorder's office and look it up yourself.

Occasionally, these legal notices of default omit the exact street address of the subject property. If this is the case, you can get the correct address by consulting the map books available while you're at the county recorder's office. Match the legal description given with the addresses in the map books.

Another source for the majority of this vital information about the default is preliminary title reports from a title company. Needless to say, ordering such reports is quite expensive. And if you examine the records available at no expense at the county recorder's office, you can gain the experience necessary to be an expert in this field.

Once you obtain needed information about a distressed property and you visit the property, you'll note an interesting phenomenon. Property in foreclosure, 99 times out of 100, has the same appearance. You can spot the neglected property a mile away. It's the only house on the block with a dried out, unmowed lawn with debris scattered about. You may notice a broken window or two, possibly a roof in need of repair, and it may require some paint. These "tattered ladies" stand out in the neighborhood like a pair of polka-dot tennis shoes worn with a tuxedo.

At one time, the trustee would offer necessary information about the default to the public as a professional courtesy. Unfortunately, this service is not given so freely anymore, due to the increasing popularity of this interesting field among speculators. Today, the trustee is only obligated to provide information for date, time, and location of sale.

CHOOSE A TERRITORY IN WHICH TO OPERATE

To be efficient, you should restrict your operations to a specific area within your city. An appropriate area is the neighborhood in which you live. The major reasons for working within a certain designated area are to develop contacts in that area and to get to know property values so that you can quickly ascertain market value in order to expedite sale. The area you select should have potential for growth, which will eventually lead to an increase in property values.

Once you have selected the territory, you can begin accumulating data relevant to events occurring in the area. Get a large map of the area and then note sales prices of homes, locations of schools, and specific streets where resales offer higher dollars per square foot of house. Additionally you can note areas that show signs of reduced value, possibly due to crime, poor land planning, or traffic congestion.

When you have become a specialist in this territory, you no longer have to confine your activities to single-family residences. Get to know values of income property, raw acreage, and industrial projects.

Limit your territory to an area not to exceed 2,000 homes. You can obtain a large map of the area from the county assessor's or county clerk's office. As trends and events occur, note them on your map in pencil. Include positive or negative trends and events that may have an economic impact on your designated territory.

PREPARE A LIST OF POTENTIAL INVESTMENTS

Listing potential investments begins with narrowing down the total supply of available distressed property from the information you have compiled. Start with all available Real Estate Owned from your meetings with REO managers. Then compile available property through the sources mentioned earlier: legal publications, subscription services, and the county recorder's office.

Compile all pertinent data on each property on the property information sheet (see sample on the following pages). This form lists all the vital information you will need to make a financial analysis and close the deal effectively.

You can develop additional potential investments while becoming acquainted with your specific territory. If you are alert, you can often spot signs of property that will eventually be in a distressed condition. Run-down homes with debris scattered about are usually rented out by absentee landlords. Due to varying circumstances, they are often abandoned by the tenants, and the absentee landlord should be contacted immediately to procure a sale. Absentee landlords who own vacated property often board up the windows and doors to protect their property from vandals. If you spot a boarded home that is not already on your list, find out who the owner is and try to make a deal.

Property Information Sheet Lot No. _____ Block No. _____
Map Page No. _____________

Owner's name: ______________________________
Property address: ______________________________
Phone: (Home) ________________ (Work) ____________
Date default action taken: _______ Final date to correct: _______

First loan
Lender's name: ________________ Loan no.: ____________
Type: _________ Is it assumable? _________
Rate of interest: _________
Original principal owing: ________ Balance as of: _______
Is _________ Monthly payments _________
Annual taxes _________

Second loan
Lender's name: ________________ Loan no.: ____________
Type: _________ Is it assumable? _________
Rate of interest: _________
Original principal owing: ________ Balance as of: _______
Is _________ Monthly payments _________
Annual taxes _________

Payments in arrears
First loan ______ No. of months at ________ = ________
Second loan ______ No. of months at ________ = ________
Third loan ______ No. of months at ________ = ________
Total late charges = ________
Total default and foreclosure fees = ________
Total amount in arrears as of ____________
Description of other liens
1. ____________ as of ______ total owing
including penalties ________
2. ____________ as of ______ total owing
including penalties ________

Sq. footage of livable area __________ Lot size __________
No. of bedrooms ____ No. of baths ____
Dining ____ Garage ____
Estimated cost to repair interior (describe rooms & work required) ______________________________

____

Total estimated cost of interior and exterior: ____________
Property location factors (good, average, below average): ____________
Lot: ________ Shopping ________ Public transportation____
Schools ________ Parks & other ________ Freeways ______

Preliminary cost estimates
Total cost of all delinquencies = ________
Title and escrow expenses = ________
Loan transfer or origination fee = ________
1 month's P&I and taxes and insurance = ________
Cash required for additional liens = ________
Total cash required to make current = ________
Total interior and exterior repair costs = ________

PREPARE AN INVESTMENT ANALYSIS

Now that you have listed potential investments, it is time to prepare a financial analysis of those that deserve further consideration. From the property information sheet, you can gather more detailed information and note it on this form.

Reason for the default, date of the default notice, final date to correct the default, and all necessary financial data, plus a range of what the property would be worth in good condition should be noted. This will prepare you to contact the owner.

MEET AND NEGOTIATE WITH THE OWNER

Keep in mind at all times that the purpose of your visit to the property is not only to aid the troubled owner in his distressed situation, but also to make a good deal for yourself. If everything goes according to the plan, the troubled owner will receive cash for his equity, and his credit will be salvaged, while you acquire title to the property.

Refrain from using the phone until you have actually met with the owner. This will avoid the potential of the troubled owner brushing you off easily over the phone. A personal visit not only is more businesslike, but it will also offer you the opportunity of looking over the home.

Begin your approach with a simple introduction of who you are and why you're there, suggesting a mood of mutual assistance. Mention that you have discovered through your sources that the property might be for sale. If in fact the property is for sale, you can immediately get into the details of the transaction. However, should the troubled owner not currently have the property up for sale, you must use a different approach.

Time is definitely of the essence in dealing with property in foreclosure.

The Time Element in Distressed Property. Bear in mind that investment in foreclosure property is a patient business. There is a great deal of effort, analysis of pertinent data, and continuing effort in order to keep abreast of available opportunities.

Remember, time is on the side of you, the investor. The pressure is on the distressed owner to remedy the situation, or else he will lose the property and his good credit rating.

It is to your advantage to remind the distressed homeowner that you're interested in making a good deal for yourself, while at the same time helping the owner realize some cash and salvage his credit rating.

During the periods of stress these distressed homeowners face during foreclosure proceedings, it is important for you to remember that they often disguise the truth about certain matters. Understandably, the loss of home and property is stressful. Therefore, it is imperative that all details of what the distressed homeowner says be verified. While you're in the presence of the homeowner, it is essential for you to keep the dialogue going to find out as much as possible about the owner's financial condition and the house.

Should the distressed owner miraculously remedy his financial condition and bring delinquent payments up to date, be happy for him. But at the same time continue to keep in touch, because now the homeowner is faced with an additional problem: how to keep up with the existing house payments plus paying back the additional funds borrowed to remedy the initial crisis. Chances are, if you continue to keep in touch, the opportunity to make a deal on the property will arise once again.

The following are suggested openings you can use to stimulate negotiations with the distressed owner:

> "If you'll allow me to make a complete financial analysis of the property, I can be back within 24 hours with a firm offer that will solve your current dilemma."
>
> "By assisting you during these troubled times, I can help myself at the same time."
>
> "I can operate much faster than a real estate agent, plus save you a costly sales commission."
>
> "I completely understand how you feel. By allowing me to acquire your property, you can be sure that the lender, or anyone else, cannot profit from your hard luck."
>
> "My purpose in being here is to offer you cash for your equity, which you would lose in a foreclosure sale. Therefore,

by dealing with me you can salvage your good credit, drive away much better off, and start all over again."

"Please allow me to see the documents on your home. Do you have the deed, the title policy, and the payment record?"

"Be careful you do not let other people know that we are speaking about a deal. If brokers and lenders get involved, it could make our deal very messy."

It is important at the onset of negotiations that the owner is made aware that time is of the essence. Since the owner is in the midst of a foreclosure proceeding, take care that the deal is completed before it is too late.

Often, during the initial stages of negotiating, a troubled owner might mention that he's arranging new financing on his distressed property. He somehow believes that the current situation can be alleviated by acquiring additional funds. The important point for you to remember is that when a house is in foreclosure, it's unlikely that the owner will be able to acquire additional financing. It is unlikely lenders would underwrite an additional loan with the current loan(s) in default. Since the owner cannot make payments on the first loan, he probably won't be able to make payments on another loan either.

If by chance the owner is able to get a loan from someone else, he's probably only postponing the inevitable foreclosure, because he now has to maintain additional payments on top of the loan he is already in default on.

Should the distressed owner state that he is arranging another loan, advise him like this: "OK, if you feel supplemental funds will ease your distressed situation, then by all means do it. But if you cannot arrange the loan, or if you have problems later, please call me so that I may present an offer for your house and assist in rectifying your credit."

The important point at this time is to leave the owner with a positive view of you, as an investor who wants to help, so that if he gets into a distressed situation again, he knows who to call.

As a professional investor, you can act faster and offer more results to a distressed owner than anyone else. The real estate agent who gets involved in the transaction requires the expense of a sizable commission, which is a needless expense when you, the private investor, purchase the property. Should government agencies get involved, they'll require expensive repairs and timely applications to be filled out before money will be refunded.

The Best Prospect in Town. A run-down house will always be the best deal in town. In fact, the more run-down, the better. Every defect in the condition of a home offers opportunity to the wise distressed-property investor. Each defect must be noted, then a minimum and maximum price must be estimated to correct each defect. Then the deal with the distressed owner is made on the basis of the maximum estimated repair cost plus a good profit for the investor. Once the property is acquired, make every effort to refurbish the property at a price as close to the minimum cost estimate as possible.

You need not be a jack-of-all-trades and fix everything personally, but it is essential that you be accurate at discovering problems and know how much it will cost to repair each problem. Then, you must know what the reconditioned home will sell for in that particular neighborhood. It is obviously foolish to invest in a property if the total cost of refurbishment is greater than its market value.

It would be a good practice to know a contractor who can walk through a home with you and determine the soundness of such items as the roof, overall plumbing, and foundation. Be thorough in your initial examinations. After a time and a few walk-throughs with someone you've hired to inspect, you will gain enough experience to make the same analysis yourself.

By thoroughly checking out the entire property, carefully analyzing it, then honestly evaluating the sales price once work is completed, you can rest assured that the risk has been minimized and a profit will be realized. If you have analyzed the numbers carefully, and the total costs of refurbishment are more than the resale value, don't entirely maroon the project. Go back to the troubled owner and reopen negotiations. Point out that it is necessary for you to make a reasonable profit. If you're still unable to make a good deal for yourself, then it's time to pack your bags. Chances are that if you keep in touch every three months or so, the same owner will be faced with financial difficulty once again. Keep the information you've compiled filed away because it may be useful someday.

ESTIMATE THE COSTS

About the easiest way to acquire a property in foreclosure is to assume the existing loan while making up all loan payments in arrears, then purchasing the deed from the owner, and finally taking possession. Very neat and clean. But, more often than not, you will have to involve yourself with details that tend to complicate matters involving distressed property. To simplify matters, use the cost estimate sheet on the next page. It considers all items involved when investing in foreclosed property. To eliminate potential errors, write down all costs.

Purchasing the Deed. Make certain that the seller has the property vested in his name by checking the grant deed or the title insurance policy. If neither of these is available, check the escrow documents when the owner purchased the property. If none of these are available for verification, check the official records at the county recorder's office.

You must know the difference between a grant deed and a quitclaim deed. An owner of real property who issues a grant deed is warranting that he has marketable title to the property. A quitclaim deed simply releases any interest the grantor may have in the property. A grantor who has no interest in the property is not releasing anything. For example, assume you give me a quitclaim deed on the

Cost Estimate Sheet

Address ______________________________

Cost of acquiring property:
- Purchasing the deed $________
- Delinquent taxes ________
- Bonds and assessments ________
- Delinquencies on first loan:
  ____ months @ $____ ________
- Total late charges and fees ________
- Advances ________
- Pay off second loan (include all delinquencies, advances, and fees) ________

Preliminary cost estimates:
- Title and escrow expenses ________
- Loan transfer or origination fee ________
- 1 month's P&I and taxes and insurance ________

Total cash to purchase: ________

- Balance of all loans after purchase ________
- Other encumbrances ________

Total property cost (before repairs) ________

Cost of repairs needed:

Paint ________	Plumbing ________	Roof ________
Electrical ________	Termite ________	Fencing ________
Landscape ________	Floors ________	Carpeting ________
Wallpaper ________	Fixtures ________	Hardware ________

Total cost of repairs ________

Total property cost (after repairs) ________

Brooklyn Bridge. If you have no interest in the Brooklyn Bridge whatsoever, you are simply executing a statement saying, "I have no interest whatsoever in the Brooklyn Bridge." Obviously you have no interest in it, and you are releasing nothing. If you accept a quitclaim deed, it is imperative that the grantor have an interest to convey to you.

Real Estate Taxes. Only rarely are delinquent property taxes assessed against a property; occasionally up to three years' worth could have accumulated. This is often the case when the lender fails to provide for an *impound account* for hazard insurance and property taxes. With an impound account, the borrower pays a prorated share of these expenses monthly into a trust out of which the lender pays these liabilities. If you are dealing with properties that have VA or FHA loans on them, you can be assured that the taxes are fairly up to date, because these government-backed loans provide for an impound account.

The best method of making sure that property taxes have been paid is to get the information directly from your county tax collector. All that is required is a simple phone call if you can supply the tax collector with the complete legal description of the subject property. If that is not available, you will have to visit the county tax collector in person.

Bonds and Assessments. Most frequently, bonds and assessments show up in less than fully developed areas where sewers and sidewalks have not been completed. Be very careful of these liens against real property because they do not always appear on the title report. These liens are recorded against real property and are written in a way to allow the homeowner to pay them off monthly over a period of years. However, in some cases, these bonds and assessments have to be fully paid off when the property is sold.

To verify whether any bonds or assessments are outstanding, or to learn any other details about them, call the tax department of the county treasurer.

Existing Loans. Probably the most important consideration in purchasing a property in foreclosure is the existing loan, or secondary loans, if any. Because there are a variety of ways the property could have been financed, you should be familiar with all the financing methods that were described in Chapter 1.

VA and FHA loans offer the foreclosure investor much more latitude than do conventional loans. This is mainly because these loans can easily be assumed by the new buyer without any qualification whatsoever; as opposed to some conventional loans, the existing interest rate is maintained, rather than adjusted upward to reflect the current market rate of interest. Furthermore, these loans seldom impose a prepayment penalty if the loan is at least two years old.

When you deal with property that has a VA or FHA loan attached, it will be much easier for you to take over the existing financing. If the property you are interested in has a conventional loan on it, you will be faced with negotiating directly with the lender. Often, conventional lenders will charge a 1 to 2 percent assumption fee on the unpaid balance. Also, they will probably adjust the interest rate upward to equal the current market rate of interest.

Conventional lenders vary substantially in their methods of handling delinquencies. However, they normally are much more strict about allowing a borrower to fall in arrears. They will usually record a notice of default if the borrower falls 60 to 90 days overdue. VA and FHA lenders usually are more patient with the borrower and often wait up to six months before recording a notice of default.

Additionally, conventional lenders normally charge higher late charges on a delinquent loan than does the VA or FHA. These late charges can run as high as 0.1 percent per month on the unpaid balance.

The law provides the borrower a period of reinstatement of the loan, meaning that within a certain period the loan can be reinstated (brought up to date), when all monies in arrears plus all penalties are paid in full. The period of reinstatement varies from state to state.

When a homeowner allows a home loan to go into arrears to the extent that the lender records a notice of default and foreclosure proceedings begin, the homeowner is usually required to pay a sizable sum to make the loan current. Because the amount is substantial, the homeowner will probably have to sell or allow the lender to foreclose.

Therefore, if you invest in a property that has a VA or FHA loan attached, you'll benefit from the following:

- You can assume the existing loan without credit qualification.
- You can assume the existing loan for a small incidental fee.
- You won't be charged a prepayment penalty when you sell.
- The interest rate will remain the same throughout the term of the loan.
- You can allow the next buyer to assume all the same benefits.

If you invest in a property that has a conventional loan with a due-on-sale clause, you'll have to:

- Be prepared to qualify for the loan;
- Possibly pay a higher rate of interest if the existing rate is substantially below the market rate;
- Pay a prepayment penalty when you sell;
- Be prepared to pay off the existing loan or get a new loan if the lender decides to exercise the due-on-sale clause.

GATHER ALL THE DATA

What do you do after you have located a property that appears profitable, obtained an appraisal, and arrived at a price range you're prepared to offer? The next step is to answer the following questions:

- What are the names of the mortgagor and mortgagee or the trustor, trustee, and lender (beneficiary)?
- Is the loan in foreclosure a first or a second loan?

- When was it recorded and for how much?
- Does a second mortgage exist?
- If the loan in foreclosure is a second loan, who holds the first?
- Is the loan a conventional loan or a government loan that can easily be assumed?
- How much is each loan in arrears?
- Are the taxes delinquent, and if so, how much?
- Are there other liens against the property?

You can find answers to most of these questions in the office of the county recorder where the subject property is located. All documentation involved with real property is kept open to the public in the county recorder's office.

The recording process dates back to before the Civil War. Now, as it did then, it provides to the public a notice of important documentation in regard to real property. When it comes time to develop data on a property in foreclosure, note that a first mortgage recorded has priority over liens that are recorded subsequently. In other words, except for tax liens, the first in line is first in right to any claims on the property.

The actual recording is done by the county recorder. When a deed is recorded, the county recorder will file a copy of that deed in the official records.

CLOSING THE DEAL

Before the distressed owner will be ready to make a deal, you must set the stage. The owner has to be convinced that you are a knowledgeable specialist in the field of real estate. You will accomplish this during the initial stage of negotiations by demonstrating knowledge about the foreclosure process and revealing to the owner exactly what will occur if the condition is not remedied. You also inform the owner that time is of the essence, that it is too late to list the property with a brokerage firm and possibly even too late to borrow additional funds. You can add that, by selling to you now, the owner will relieve his distressed condition, salvage his good credit rating, and be able to leave the burdensome property behind with some cash in hand. Otherwise, the lender will acquire the property and everything will be lost, including the owner's credit rating and accumulated equity.

The distressed owner should appreciate the investor's interest and be relieved that help is near at hand. Owners feel they can speak openly when the limits of their financial difficulties are out in the open. For that reason, the owner no longer feels someone is intruding, and he has no need to disguise the facts about his troubled financial condition.

Now the distressed owner is prepared to act. Time is running out, and he has been alerted to the consequences. The owner knows that you can remedy the situation better and faster than anyone else. Now the owner is ready to make a deal.

Price Declines with Time. Time is money. In no other field of business can this truism be stated more emphatically. During the typical 90-day span of a foreclosure proceeding, during which a property can still be reinstated, offers to the owner will vary. An offer during the first 30 days would be considerably higher than an offer made during the final days of redemption. During the final days of the redemption period, the offer would be at its lowest.

By the time a property reaches the final days of the 90-day period of reinstatement, additional unpaid monthly installments have accumulated, and late charges have increased. The owner must be alerted to these facts; the more quickly the owner acts to resolve the problem, the more he will get out of it.

Make Sure the Names Are Correct. It is imperative that all sellers' names on the deed are correct and that all the information on the deed transferring the property exactly matches that on the original deed the seller received from the lending institution. If the seller's legal signature is Andrew J. McLean, it is necessary to put down the name exactly as it is shown, not Andy McLean or A. McLean. Errors often occur when information is copied from published information on the original grant deed.

Once the owner has signed over the grant deed, you should immediately take it to the recording office and have it recorded. After recordation, submit a copy of the grant deed to the title company. Immediately recording the grant deed assures you that any liens recorded against your newly acquired property will be invalid, as long as they are recorded behind your name, and not before.

First you must have the seller sign the equity purchase agreement, which will give you, the buyer, control of the subject property. This will be accomplished after completing final negotiations and checking that the property is actually transferable. Then the grant deed can be executed, signed by the owners, and properly notarized. Again, be sure that the grant deed is filled out exactly as the previous grant deed. Once the grant deed is properly executed and notarized, it must be taken to the county recorder for recordation.

The sample Equity Purchase Agreement shown on pages 62 and 63 should help you when it comes time to negotiate with a distressed owner.

Investing in Real Estate Owned

REO is property that has been foreclosed and that failed to sell at public auction. The bank or savings and loan institution now owns the property. One aspect of REO that makes it a superior investment compared to the other two stages of foreclosure is what the lender does for you. In the process of acquiring the property, the bank or other institution will clear it of outstanding liens, conduct necessary title searches, and pay back taxes. The lender owns the property free and clear. If you can acquire REO property, it will be free of problems, except deferred maintenance.

There are other advantages to investing in REO property. You can usually buy REO with a small down payment. You can usually finance your purchase at interest rates that are below market rates, since the lending institution itself is also the seller and is eager to unload the property. It is often possible to defer the first principal and interest payment until one to six months after the acquisition of the property. Finally, the bank will usually handle most of the closing costs.

To succeed in investing in REO, you must find a technique for dealing with the bankers who own it. This can be difficult because there is a lot of public interest in the purchase of foreclosure property, and potential buyers are constantly inquiring.

Typically, an inquiry from an uninformed member of the public is in the form of phone calls to various banks, asking if any foreclosure property is available. So many people phone in that the banks now usually give a stock reply: sorry, nothing available.

REO will usually be moved through an established real estate broker, directly to known buyers, or even to personal friends of the banker. Thus, if you want to invest in REO, it is your job to approach the REO department in person, and to meet its manager. Establishing such a personal relationship at a lending institution is the only viable way to get into the REO business.

Equity Purchase Agreement

(This agreement to be filled out in triplicate, with one copy going to the seller, one copy to the buyer, and one copy to the buyer's file records.)

Date ______________ Address of subject property______________
Lot ______________ Block ______________ Tract ______________
Lender's name ______________ Loan number ______________
Seller's name ______________ Address ______________
Buyer's name ______________ Address ______________

Buyer agrees to purchase and Seller agrees to sell the equity in the above described real property for the sum of ______________ net to the seller, receipt of which is hereby acknowledged by the Seller.

Buyer agrees to take title to the above described property subject only to existing liens and encumbrances not exceeding ______________.

It is also mutually agreed that: ______________.

Seller is to deliver possession of subject property on or before ______________, 19_____. If the property is not transferred to the buyer by the above agreed date, all payments and further expenses incurred from that date forward shall be deducted from the net amount to the Seller.

Buyer will pay all escrow, title, loan transfer, and closing costs.

Monthly payments on the above loan including, principal, interest, taxes, and insurance are ______________.

Impounds for taxes and insurance, if any, are to be assigned without charge to the buyer. Any unforeseen shortage in the impound account will be deducted from the net amount due Seller at closing.

Seller will immediately execute a Grant Deed in favor of Buyer, which the Buyer has the right to record.

Seller will not remove any fixtures from the real property and will leave property reasonably clean and in good condition.

Seller will allow Buyer access to subject property for any reason prior to date of possession of the Buyer.

Buyer will pay the balance of all funds due Seller at closing after checking title, loans, and liens, and the property is vacated.

Additions to this agreement: ______________________________
____
____

Buyer ______________________ Seller ______________________
Buyer ______________________ Seller ______________________

4
Appraisal

Appraisal is of primary importance to your potential success at investing. Due to the fact that you will be buying undervalued property, fixing it up, then reselling at market value, you must be accurate at determining value. Without proper appraisal techniques you can be burdened with the major pitfall of real estate investment—that of paying too much for investment property.

THE TECHNICAL DEFINITION

An appraisal of real estate is an opinion, or estimate, of a property's value, made by gathering and analyzing the essential data as of a specific date. The appraisal is based upon the highest and best use of that property, the use that will produce the greatest net return. Such an estimate must consider zoning laws, government regulations, and the demand for that type of property in that area.

Appraisal of real estate is an art, not a science; the appraiser is actually arriving at a range of values within which the subject property may be expected to sell. Although three different appraisers may come up with three different opinions of value, these opinions will probably fall within a close range.

PROFESSIONAL METHODS OF APPRAISAL

Real property is appraised by various methods: market data, reproduction cost, and capitalization. The final opinion of value is given by weighing the values from each method used.

Market Data Method

The most widely used method of appraisal is the market data, or comparable sales, approach. This method compares the subject property with comparable properties recently sold in the area. The value of the subject property is adjusted upward or downward according to amenities, construction type, quality, and individual location.

A simple application of the comparable sales approach would be to compare the subject property with three properties that have sold within six months, are located within the same tract, and have essentially no meaningful differences. Assume all these comparables have sold for between $50,000 and $51,000, and that the subject property has a swimming pool while the comparables do not. You determine that a swimming pool is worth $10,000; therefore the subject property is worth approximately $61,000 ($51,000 plus $10,000 for the pool). This method is primarily used for appraising condominiums and single family residences.

Reproduction Cost Method

The reproduction cost, or replacement cost, method has three steps:

1. Determine today's cost of replacing all improvements on the property.
2. Deduct depreciation to determine the current appraised value of the improvements.

3. Add the current value of the improvements to the value of the land.

For an example, assume that the subject property consists of a standard brick home on a 60′ × 150′ lot, and the home is 30 years old. If today's construction costs are $35 per square foot and the subject property contains 1,500 square feet of living space, it would cost 1,500 × $35 or $52,500 to replace the improvement (the house). Now you must deduct the depreciation from that cost. If the value of the house has depreciated $3,000, then the current appraised value of the improvement is $52,500 less $3,000, or $49,500. If comparable vacant lots (unimproved property) in that area are currently selling for $10,000, then your total appraised value of the subject property is $49,500 plus $10,000, or $59,500.

The reproduction cost method is predominantly used when appraising service properties such as public buildings, schools, and hospitals, and fairly new buildings of all types where the depreciation is a minor factor in the overall appraisal.

Capitalization or Income Method

The capitalization, or income, approach to the appraisal of real property is primarily used to determine value of income property. To understand this approach, you must first understand cash flow—your monthly net income from a property.

Cash flow comes in two forms, positive and negative. It is the amount of actual cash an investor will receive after deducting operating expenses and debt service. Usually, the amount of cash flow an investor receives from a property will depend upon the down payment, or equity invested in the property, and whether that property is prime or lower-income.

For an example, I will use my first real estate investment made many years ago. I purchased a three-bedroom, one-bath single-family residence for $13,400, with a $1,500 down payment. It wasn't much of a house, actually—it seemed as though there were only a couple of inches between my house and the ones next door, the garage wouldn't accommodate a late-model lawn mower, the wiring was substandard, and everything needed new paint.

I painted the whole place myself and hired an electrician to upgrade the wiring. All in all, I spent about $500 fixing it up. Then I rented the house to three bachelors for $240 per month. My total monthly payment, including principal and interest, taxes and insurance, was $138. Thus, before vacancy allowance and repair expense I cleared $102 per month, every month the house was rented.

Gross annual rent (12 months @ $240)	$2,880
Less: Vacancy (5%)	– 144
Gross annual rent after vacancy	2,736
Less: Repair and maintenance (5%)	144
Less: Taxes and insurance	480
Total operating expenses	624
Net operating income	2,112
Less: Annual debt service (12 months @ $102)	1,224
Cash flow before taxes	888

The capitalization method of appraisal uses the net operating income (NOI) to arrive at a fair market value for the property. To arrive at net operating income, first calculate the gross income (based upon 100 percent rentals), and then deduct operating expenses, including potential losses from bad debts and vacancy.

The income appraisal technique also depends upon what the appraiser considers a suitable rate of return for investment capital in that area. Obviously, if you are investing in a high-risk area (such as a lower-income neighborhood) you must receive a higher return on your investment. Conversely, prime property carries a lower risk factor and thus a lower rate of return.

This rate of return on invested capital is called the capitalization or "cap" rate, and must be arbitrarily determined by the appraiser. The cap rate normally varies from 8 percent in the best neighborhoods to 12 percent in high-risk areas, but this percentage must be adjusted based upon the going rate for that type of property. The appraiser determines the rate within the 8 to 12 percent range by considering the risk of the investment, along with the type of property and the quality of the income.

In our example, we determined that NOI was $2,112. We estimate an average cap rate of 10 percent, because the subject property is neither a slum nor prime property. Now we simply divide the cap rate into the NOI, or $2,112 divided by 0.10 yields an approximate appraised value of $21,120.

Appraisal by Gross Income Multiplier

Appraisal by gross income multiplier is a fast and simple way of determining an approximate value of a property, with respect to its gross income. This method of determining value cannot be classed as a professional approach, but brokers often use it as a quick, off-the-cuff calculation and to compare with similar properties in advertisements. Often, in newspaper ads for income properties, you will see a sales price given as "8 times the gross." This means that the sales price of that particular property is 8 times the gross income (income before deductions of expenses). For example, if gross income is $20,000, then the selling price would be $20,000 times 8, or $160,000. In this case, 8 is the gross income multiplier.

As with capitalization rate, the gross income multiplier is determined by the appraiser within a range of values, considering the "going rate" for the area. This going rate is normally between 4 and 12, where the lower number represents the less desirable locations.

If the gross income equals $20,000 per year:

	Multiplier	**Value**
Worst area	4	$80,000
Average area	7	$140,000
Best area	11	$220,000

The gross income multiplier is mostly used as an immediate gauge to determine whether a property deserves further attention. It gives only a ball-park estimate, it does not reflect net income, and it is unreliable for arriving at a true value.

APPRAISING ON YOUR OWN

Market Analysis

Remember, appraisal of real property is an art, not a science. The important ability is to know good value, and the only way to do that is to *know the market.* If you know the market and are fully informed about what properties in the neighborhood are selling for, then you can determine what a good buy is.

The Market Analysis Form on the following page can assist you in noting important data that will eventually help you in making your final appraisal. Note the column labeled Price/Sq. Ft. In this column, you will enter the price per square foot that particular house sold for. (As of this writing, the average cost per square foot to build new residential housing was $40 per square foot for average quality and $50 per square foot to build a custom home.)

You will have to know costs of repair and replacement items, such as carpeting, painting, tiling, and replacing broken windows. This information is very important because you must be able to look at a dumpy old house,

Market Analysis Form

Subject property address ______________________________ Date ____________

Information on similar properties in same general area that may have same approximate value.

Currently for sale

Address	Bedrooms	Baths	Den/ Fam.rm.	Sq.ft.	Price/ Sq.ft.	Mortgages	Interest rate	Days on market

Sold within last six months

Address	Bedrooms	Baths	Den/ Fam.rm.	Sq.ft.	Price/ Sq.ft.	Mortgages	Interest rate	Days on market

estimate the cost to repair it and the amount you can sell it for, and do all that sometimes in less than an hour.

As a good rule of thumb, you want every dollar of fix-up cost to equal two dollars in increased value. In other words, if you spend $1,000 fixing it up, you then would want the overall value of the house to go up twice as much, or $2,000 more in value.

The cost per square foot is probably the most important factor in analyzing a property. When you do a market analysis of a particular neighborhood, especially study the cost per square foot. Doing so will help you quickly determine basic values in that neighborhood.

Financial Analysis

The major element in finding a good buy is financial analysis. Let us examine a single-family residence that was purchased and lease-optioned and see how it operates. The figures are actual, and the principles used will apply to both SFRs and multi-unit buildings. Our example is a house purchased for $37,000 with a $4,500 down payment and $1,500 to fix it up. The tenant pays $400 per month rent plus $150 per month option fee. The tenant has option to purchase at $49,000 with $3,000 down (including option fees), balance payable at 12 percent for 20 years.

OPERATING STATEMENT

The Income Property Operating Statement on pages 72–73 shows the data needed to analyze the property.

The following list explains the numbered items:

1. **Gross scheduled rental income:** Total annual rent the property would receive at 100 percent occupancy.
2. **Other income:** Additional income, such as coin-operated washer and dryer.
3. **Total gross income:** Total of all money collected from the operation of the building.

Income Property Operating Statement

Name Biltmore **Date** 3-12-81 **Price** $37,000

Address 635 Biltmore **Loan #1** $15,000 **Loan #2** $17,500

Type SFR **Description** 2 bedroom, 1 bath **Loan #3** ______ **Equity** $4,500

Rented @ $400 plus $150 option fee

Assessed Value

Land	$2,000	20%
Improvements	$8,000	80%

Financing

	Balance owed	Monthly pymt.	Interest	Term
Existing				
1st	$15,000	$125	7%	15 yr.
2nd	$17,500	$144	10%	10 yr.
3rd				
Potential				
1st	$46,000		12%	20 yr.
2nd				

Item No.	Item	%		Amount	Comments
1	Gross scheduled rental income			$4,800	$400 × 12
2	Plus: Other income			1,800	option fee
3	Total gross income			6,600	

4	Less: Vacancy and credit losses	5%		240	
5	Gross operating income			6,360	
6	Less: Operating expenses				
7	Property taxes		$180		
8	Property insurance		120		
9	Property management				
10	Utilities				
11	License and advertising	1%	48		
12	Repairs and maintenance	5%	240		
13	Trash removal				
14	Supplies				
15	Gardener and pool service				
16	Total operating expenses			588	
17	Net operating income			5,772	
18	Less: Annual debt service			3,228	
19	Cash flow before taxes			2,544	
20	Plus: Equity buildup			420	
21	Gross equity income			2,964	
22	Less: Depreciation			2,960	
23	Taxable income			4	

Note: Depreciation is determined by using 80% of purchase price then 10% (ACRS 12 years)

4. **Vacancy and credit losses:** Use 5 percent of the gross scheduled rental income. That's the national average.
5. **Gross operating income:** Total income this property should generate in a year's time after vacancy and credit losses are deducted.
6. **Operating expenses:** Normal expenses incurred during the year are deducted from gross operating income. The operating expenses include property taxes, insurance, property management, utilities, license and advertising, repairs and maintenance, trash removal, supplies, gardener, and pool service.
7. **Property taxes:** Annual real property taxes are entered here. In many cases monthly tax and insurance costs are part of the monthly mortgage payment paid into an impound account. You can usually get monthly or annual tax information from the mortgage statement. If not, you can determine what your current tax bill will be by calling the county tax assessor and asking for the tax assessment for the current year.
8. **Property insurance:** This is the total amount for all necessary forms of insurance. You could assume the seller's existing policy, but it is wiser to check out other policies because the property may be underinsured and rates vary substantially.
9. **Property management:** If you plan to manage the property yourself, you need not enter a figure here. Otherwise, include an annual cost figure, including cost of the resident manager. Surveys indicate that a reasonable salary to pay a resident manager is a range of $5 to $17 per month per unit in the building. Professional management companies are paid 5 to 10 percent of actual rents to oversee the entire property.
10. **Utilities:** An annual figure including gas, water, and electricity.
11. **License and advertising:** Use actual figures for advertising and license fee cost for the entire year.

12. **Repairs and maintenance:** This item covers a reserve fund for replacement of furniture, drapes, carpets, and all major equipment (elevators, water heaters, etc.). A fair estimate is 5 percent of gross scheduled rental income.

13, 14, & 15. Reserved for particular expense items that may occur on properties.

16. **Total operating expenses:** Total expenses before debt service. As a rule of thumb, this figure is usually within a range of 30 to 50 percent of gross collected rents, with 40 percent being average. A higher percentage is used for older buildings and a lower percentage for newer buildings.
17. **Net operating income:** The result of deducting total operating expenses from gross operating income. This figure represents what the property would earn if purchased for cash free and clear of any loans. This item is also used to determine a capitalized value by dividing a suitable cap rate into the net operating income.
18. **Annual debt service:** The annual total of payments including principal and interest.
19. **Cash flow before taxes:** The result of deducting annual debt service from net operating income, or the actual cash you'll have left over after expenses and debt service.
20. **Equity buildup:** The portion of the annual debt service that applies toward principal payoff of the loan.
21. **Gross equity income:** The result of adding annual equity payments to cash flow before taxes.
22. **Depreciation:** As a general rule, 80 percent of the property's value can be depreciated for income tax purposes; the remaining 20 percent is allocated to the land, which cannot be depreciated. (See the special section on depreciation and tax savings, Chapter 10.)

23. **Taxable income:** The result of deducting depreciation from gross equity income.

The Income Property Operating Statement is important because the numbers predict how much you're going to make. Some of the more important items on the operating statement are the operating expenses, net operating income, cash flow before taxes, and taxable income. Operating expenses are usually about 40 percent of gross scheduled rental income for the average building. For older buildings, these expenses can be figured at 37 percent due to lower maintenance costs. For much older buildings, operating expenses can run about 43 percent due to higher costs of repair and maintenance.

Net operating income (NOI) is important because it is the figure capitalized to appraise income property. If the NOI is $5,000 and the cap rate is 10 percent, you would divide the NOI by the cap rate to determine value. In this case the result would be a value of $50,000. If a cap rate of 12 percent is used, the resulting appraised value would be $41,667 ($5,000 divided by 12 percent).

Cash flow before taxes is the actual amount of money you will net every year after all expenses and debt service are deducted. You definitely want this figure to be positive so you won't have to come up with cash out of your pocket to operate the property.

Finally, taxable income is the bottom line of the operating statement. It is the so-called tax shelter advantage of owning income-producing real estate. As you can see from the example, although there was $2,544 positive cash flow before taxes, the actual taxable income was only $4. In other words, you received $2,544 in net proceeds during the year on this property, but for income tax purposes you earned only $4. This is where the term "tax shelter" evolved; you are sheltering income through depreciation of income-producing real estate.

EQUITY BUILDUP/EXAMPLE

The example below shows how to determine equity buildup (paying down of principal) for the first year on an amortized loan with the following characteristics:

Loan amount	$40,000
Interest	10%
Term of loan	20 years
Monthly payment	$386

The calculations are as follows:

Total payments:	
Monthly payment of $386 × 12 months	$4,632
Interest paid:	
Loan of $40,000 × 10%	4,000
Equity Buildup:	
Total payments less interest payments	632
Loan balance at end of first year:	
Loan of $40,000 less $632	$39,368

ASSESSING RISK

Assessment of risk is based on a few facts. First of all, risk and return (profit) are closely related: the lower the risk, the lower the rate of return; conversely, the higher the risk, the greater the return and the greater the chances for loss.

Probably the lowest-risk investment you can make is opening a passbook savings account at your local savings and loan association. Your deposit would be guaranteed to $100,000 by the Federal Savings and Loan Insurance Corporation and is virtually risk-free. But look what you get for your risk-free investment, a meager 5 to 5.5 percent. That's barely keeping up with inflation, and to make matters even worse, you have to pay income taxes on the interest you earned.

Owning real estate is usually risky only when you do not follow certain guidelines. Three problem areas that lead some property owners into financial trouble are paying too much for a particular property, overextending oneself with too much debt, and deferring maintenance.

You can avoid overpaying for a property by carefully analyzing the market before you buy. Well-informed buyers know a good buy when they see one and, conversely, are fully aware if a property is overpriced.

Property owners who overextend themselves with debt usually lack an adequate financial plan. They promise to pay balloon payments at some time in the future, and when the future comes they cannot meet their obligations.

Deferred maintenance causes loss of value and rental income, because tenants avoid uninhabitable or uncomfortable units. You should keep money in reserve to maintain your buildings properly when the work is required, so they do not turn into slums. Proper maintenance allows you to keep your units full of regularly paying tenants and maintains the property value at its maximum.

Therefore, if you follow the guidelines outlined in this book, you shouldn't have any problem overcoming these inherent risks associated with owning real property.

5

Fixing Up Your Property

When I started in this business, my only training in fixing things up was a high school class titled Shop 101. As a beginning investor, I hired most of the work out until I learned how to do it myself. If I didn't learn by watching, I learned by reading. (I recommend the *Reader's Digest Complete Do-It-Yourself Manual.*)

Sometimes it's not even necessary to fix a house up. Frequently it may only need something added to make it more appealing, which in turn will make the home profitable. For example, I recently purchased a lovely custom home that actually didn't need any fixing up, but it was so plain that it showed poorly. All I really did to improve this home was add a lot of wood and a little wallpaper to make it more appealing.

This particular home was a large three-bedroom, two-and-a-half bath on a half acre. It had a very expensive carpet, still in good condition; however, this carpet was so unappealing in the sunken living room that when you first entered the house you received a poor first impression of the entire home. My wife suggested that dark hardwood floors would be nice in the living room, and I agreed. The carpet seemed nice throughout the rest of the house; it only looked unappealing in the living room. The rest of the house lacked any decorating per se, and it was done mostly in white and off-white colors.

The first thing we did was lay in hardwood floors in the living room. Wow! The wood was magnificent, and it made a great impression when you came through the entry. Next we put solid oak laid diagonally on two walls in the living room near the entry. Then we stained the oak to match the tone of the solid oak floors. The finishing touch was to encase both archways at the living room and adjacent dining room with solid oak, stained and varnished to match the gorgeous living room floors. We did the whole job ourselves, and it was truly a pleasure. My neighbors were impressed, and everybody loved all the woodwork. But the final pleasure came when I lease-optioned the house for a handsome $20,000 profit four months after I bought it. I am convinced to this day that we would never have made as much, nor had such great response, had we not added all that woodwork to that once very plain home.

HIRING A CONTRACTOR

A question you'll probably ask yourself many times is whether to do the repairs yourself or to hire the job out every time you buy a fixer-upper. That decision is based on whether or not you have adequate fix-up funds. If you have plenty of cash and are in a big hurry to invest in more property, then I would suggest hiring the work out. But, if you're like most of us, always scraping for a buck and wanting to earn some "sweat equity," then you'd be wise to do most of the work yourself. Personally, I enjoy the work. I usually hire out only the work I'm incapable of doing. When I do hire the work out, I make a point of watching what's being done and asking plenty of questions—because next time I'll do the job myself.

If you decide to hire a contractor, follow these guidelines:

1. Discuss the job you want done with at least two contractors and get written bids for the work.
2. Talk to your neighbors. Ask them if they can recommend someone. Good craftsmen build their business on their reputation. Satisfied customers will be your best guide.
3. Get at least three references from the contractor and check them out. Call each one and ask whether there were any problems; if there were, were they corrected? Also inquire into whether there were any extra charges and whether the work was completed on time.

DOING IT YOURSELF

The best fix-up properties are those that simply need cleaning up and some cosmetic work inside and out. Try to avoid those old clunkers that require a new roof, plumbing, flooring, and new concrete. These are problem areas that usually require a specialized contractor and plenty of cash. Stick with properties that require only cosmetic work, such as painting and patching.

If you had to hire a contractor to paint and patch an average-size home, it would cost you about $700 for the interior and $800 for the exterior. The same job, if you did it yourself, would cost only $60 in materials for the interior and $70 for the exterior.

Painting the Interior

Latex paints are recommended for painting the interior, because they are easy to apply, can be thinned and cleaned up with water, dry quickly, and have little or no odor. Flat latex is best for interior walls and ceilings. Semi-gloss or enamel finishes are preferred on doors, window trim and baseboards, and bathroom and kitchen walls. The semi-gloss or enamel finish will take more scrubbing and abuse than flat paints.

Recommended is an off-white color like antique white or beige. If you keep all your rentals painted in a standard color, you'll work more efficiently, avoiding partly filled paint cans of a variety of colors. Off-white makes a room appear larger than dark colors, fits nicely with most furniture schemes, and looks clean.

Careless painting wastes time and can be a real messy experience. Proper preparation is necessary to do a good job that will last the years. Your first step is purchasing all your paint and supplies. You can save money by buying five-gallon cans of paint instead of single gallons. Next wash the walls and woodwork with soap and water. (Paint adheres better to a clean, nonglossy finish.) Fill all cracks and holes with spackling. Let dry and sand down. Remove all fixtures, electrical plates, and switch covers from surfaces to be painted. Then cover everything with dropcloths to protect the furniture and the floor. Apply paint to the ceiling first, then the walls; finish up with the trim and semi-gloss work.

Landscaping

In most cases, fix-up properties will require you to dress up the front of the house to make it more appealing. Keep in mind that first impressions are lasting impressions. If a prospective tenant or buyer drives up to inspect your property and the grounds are shabby, the prospect is likely to just keep on driving without further inspection. However, if your lawn is well-maintained and tidy, the entire property will definitely deserve further attention from a prospective buyer or tenant.

Remember, it is likely that you will be holding your investment for an extended time. Therefore, it would be sensible to invest in a sprinkler system for at least the front yard, if it doesn't already have one. A total system, including grass seed, can be done for less than $500. If you decide to do the job yourself, materials will cost less than $150.

Whether you rent or lease-option your property, it is important to keep the grounds properly maintained. I would even recommend investing in a timer to turn the sprinkler system on and off so your tenant won't be left with the responsibility of watering the lawn.

GENERAL FIX-UP TIPS

Wall-to-wall carpeting gives your units a special glow of warmth and luxury. Before you go overboard, however, you must consider expenses related to return on investment. Instead of installed wall-to-wall coverage, you can keep carpeting expense to a minimum by using linoleum in the entry area and hallways, bathrooms, and at times in the dining area. Linoleum lasts much longer than carpeting and represents a significant savings.

When you do purchase carpeting, a gold or beige shag of good quality is your best value. These colors match almost any furnishings and show stains less than other kinds. Furthermore, it is best to stay with one standard color for all your units, in order to take advantage of quantity discounts. Shag carpet has an advantage over other types in being easier to patch, although it is more expensive to begin with.

The carpeting industry is highly competitive, and you will find a large number of suppliers to choose from. Shop around and get the best price. And consider using the moonlighters of the industry, who will often install a carpet for less than the cost of a package deal from a large supplier.

Finally, save all old drapes, carpets, curtains, and furniture. These items come in handy on any future rentals.

CONVERTING THE GARAGE TO A RENTAL UNIT

Consider converting a two- or three-car garage into a rental unit. You could receive $275 per month in rental income ($3,300 per year) from a garage converted to a studio apartment.

The conversion would entail removing the garage door and installing an entry door and erecting a wall. Carpeting would be needed, plus a bathroom and small kitchen area.

Total cost of such a conversion would be about $3,000, which would be returned to you within one year through rental income. Of course, a conversion of this type would be more feasible and economical if the garage walls were already finished and there were existing plumbing lines in the vicinity of the garage.

SHOULD YOU LIVE IN THE HOUSE?

Don't live in the house you're fixing up unless you and your spouse are prepared to move a lot and temporarily live in a messy house. If you and your family feel you can live the gypsy life, then by all means move in and start fixing it up, because there are plenty of advantages. It is convenient to be living in the home you're fixing up because there won't be any travel time back and forth from the job. And, once the home is all fixed up, your prospects can come directly to you, instead of you driving out to meet them at a vacant house. Finally, your home will show better to prospective buyers when it's completely furnished and lived in than will an unattended vacant house.

6

Making the Deal

You've been combing the local neighborhoods looking for a good buy, and you find one that looks promising. Now what do you do? Negotiations begin right here, but wait—probably the most important time you will ever experience buying and selling real estate is the next hour you will spend negotiating with the seller. And the first person to mention a number loses. If you're patient and wait long enough, the seller will speak of a number, weakening his position. A motivated seller becomes even more anxious in the presence of a patient negotiator.

Whatever you and the seller finally agree on (once it's in writing), you are going to have to live with for the next 20 years. So it is absolutely imperative that you're fully informed and bargain for a good deal.

PREPARING TO NEGOTIATE

Before you even start direct negotiations, you must establish the maximum dollar amount you would pay for the property. Be sure that you are fully informed of market conditions (what similar properties are selling for in today's market).

Ideally, negotiations are easier when the seller is highly motivated, wanting to sell for any of various reasons. You already know the seller's asking price and terms. Let's say the seller's asking price is $60,000. You know, from doing your homework, that similar homes in the area sell for between $52,000 and $65,000. Now you have a basis to work from.

NEGOTIATING

If at this point the seller starts negotiations with a statement like, "The least I would take is $58,000 with a $5,000 down payment," answer with silence. Now at least you know the seller is flexible. You could agree to this, but there is definitely more room for negotiation. The seller starts getting anxious and says, "Well, I guess I could take $53,000, but not a penny less." Notice that you haven't said a thing, and already the seller has knocked $7,000 off the asking price. Let the seller do the talking. The silence is working great for you and is weakening the seller's position.

Negotiation is bargaining to reach agreement. Unless you are prepared to pay all cash and at the seller's asking price, you will be bargaining price or terms. As a rule of thumb, if a seller is firm on price, then negotiate terms. If he is firm on terms, then negotiate price. If the seller is firm on neither, then you can negotiate both price and terms. If he is firm on both, then start looking for another investment (unless of course the asking price is just too good to pass up, which is unlikely).

THE FINAL ROUND: MAKING THE OFFER

At this point you have felt out the seller and have a good idea of what he needs out of the property. The figure you have in mind should be the absolute top dollar you will pay for the property; of course, anything below that figure is actually what you're attempting to establish.

Start with negotiating the price. Get the price as low as you possibly can before doing anything else. Next you negotiate the down payment and again, keep your down payment as small as possible. You need to preserve your cash to fix up the property and to buy additional properties. Your cash is important; it's working capital, and without it you're out of business. Remember the principle of leverage: the less invested in a property, the more your leverage and the greater your return on investment.

Deposit Receipt and Offer to Purchase Form

Once negotiations have been completed and the price and terms are agreed upon, then it's time to put your offer in writing. Your written offer is to be completed on the Deposit Receipt and Offer to Purchase form. An example is shown at the end of this chapter. Follow these guidelines to ensure that important information is not omitted.

AMOUNT OF EARNEST MONEY DEPOSIT

Any amount from $1 to $3,000 would be an appropriate amount for the earnest money deposit. I recommend using $100 as a deposit, so as to limit your liability. Why? Because just in case you are forced, for whatever reason, to default on the deal, you want to keep your loss to a minimum. Should your offer be accepted, it is likely that the seller, or the seller's agent, will want more of a deposit to secure the deal and protect his interest.

PAYMENT OF PURCHASE PRICE

> Buyer to sign and Seller to carry a note secured by a Second Mortgage in the amount of $________ payable at $__________ per month, or more, including interest at _____% per annum, with the entire balance due __________ years from date of note.

Here you want to keep the interest rate and monthly payments as low as possible. If there is to be a balloon payment at the end of the term of the loan, extend the due date as far into the future as you can. Short-term balloon payments are a big disadvantage; avoid them at all costs. Furthermore, do not allow the seller to include a due-on-sale clause in this note. Such a clause will severely inhibit the salability of the property.

CLOSING DATE

If you are assuming existing financing without qualification, then you usually close escrow within 30 days. Allow yourself at least 45 days if you need conventional financing. Should you purchase an occupied rental property, engineer the closing date to coincide with the date the rents are due. You are rarely obligated to pay mortgage payments until 30 days after closing, but you are entitled to collect all the rents and retain deposits on the first day of ownership.

SUBJECT-TO CLAUSES

Clauses called subject-to clauses are inserted into the offer to require certain limitations and conditions that must be fulfilled before the offer is valid. Consider the following subject-to clauses in your offer to purchase:

> Subject to buyer obtaining a new first mortgage in the amount of $________ payable at approximately $________ per month including interest at _____% per annum.

This subject-to clause limits your liability. If you don't obtain financing, you can get your deposit back.

> Subject to all equipment, including appliances, pertaining to the operation of the building being in good working order as of the day of closing.

Here the seller, not you, will have to pay for repairs, should anything go wrong before closing.

A subject-to clause can cover almost anything, and you need certain ones to limit your liability. But keep in mind that the seller's agent will attempt to eliminate excessive subject-to's, because they inhibit an easy closing.

Counteroffers

Commonly the seller will find your offer unacceptable and in most cases will propose a counteroffer. The procedure of offer/counteroffer is important because it brings out how flexible both the buyer and seller are going to be. Remember, you should have already limited the amount you will pay, and you don't want to move beyond that point. If you are confronted with an inflexible seller, don't waste any more of your time. Chalk up your time and energy to experience and go on to another project. If, on the other hand, the property remains an excellent buy, then continue to swiftly pursue an agreement. Often, especially when there is a good buy at hand, a property is sold out from underneath a negotiating buyer because he or she persisted in demanding excessive concessions from the seller.

Practice the art of negotiating and making offers. The experience will definitely enhance your future ability to make a great buy.

The following Purchase Agreement Checklist is designed to assist you in filling out all of the necessary data required on the Deposit Sheet and Offer to Purchase agreements.

Purchase Agreement Checklist

Name of prospective buyer(s) ______________________

Currently residing at ______________________

Phone ( ) ______________________

Considering purchasing the property located at ______________________

____

for a purchase price of $______________

Earnest money deposit to be held by ______________ in amount of $______________

Balance of cash (down payment) at closing $______________

Amount of mortgage required $____________________
Type of financing ____________________
Interest at __________ % for a term of ________ years
Principal and interest payments to be approximately
$____________________ per month
Real estate taxes last year were __________
Contingencies to be included in purchase
agreement: ____________________

Items included in selling price: ____________________

Items not included in selling price: ____________________

Seller will vacate the premises on __________
Date of closing escrow __________
Sellers to pay rent of $__________ per day if sellers occupy premises after the close of escrow.
Legal description of property: ____________________

Deposit Receipt and Offer to Purchase

Date: ________, 19 ____

Received from ____________________
the sum of __________ dollars ($________) in the form of
☐ cash ☐ note ☐ check to be deposited and checks presented for payment upon acceptance of this offer, to secure and apply on the purchase of the following described property:

commonly known as ____________________,
for the purchase price of __________ dollars ($________)
subject to conditions, restrictions, reservations, and rights-of-way now on record, if any. Balance of the purchase price is to be paid as follows:

It is hereby agreed:

1) That in the event the Buyer shall fail to complete the purchase as herein provided, the amount paid herewith may, at the option of the Seller, be retained as the consideration for execution of this agreement.

2) That an escrow is to be opened with ______________ or other designated escrow agent, who will be instructed to prorate current taxes, insurance, rents, sewer use fees, and interest (if any) of subject property to ______________ unless otherwise provided herein. The amount of bond assessments, if any, which is a lien or assessed against said property to become a lien, shall be ☐ paid by the Seller, or ☐ assumed by the Buyer (check one).

3) That escrow is to close on or before ______________, and possession of premises shall be given ______________.

4) That certain items of personal property, attached hereto as Exhibit "A" are included in the total purchase price as shown above and are to remain with the property.

5) That final vesting to be:

and that evidence of this title to be in the form of owner's policy of title insurance furnished by ______________ and paid for by the Seller. Escrow fees as customarily charged in the State of ______________ are to be divided equally between Buyer and Seller unless otherwise stated as required. In the event of the cancellation and/or default of this contract, the defaulting party shall be liable for all fees or charges incurred when that party is otherwise obligated to perform under this contract.

6) That this payment of earnest money is made subject to the approval of the Seller and unless so approved and communicated to the Buyer by (date-time) ______________ and subsequently delivered, the return of the money, upon demand by the Buyer, shall cancel this agreement without damages to the undersigned. In the event of a dispute between the parties regarding the disposition of the monies paid pursuant to this contract, the Broker or the designated escrow agent holding said monies shall retain possession of such funds without liability

and shall not be obligated to dispose of those funds until there is an agreement between the parties, or by court order to do so.

7) It is understood and agreed that the terms written in this Offer and Receipt constitute the entire contract between the Buyer and Seller and that no oral statements made by the Broker, relative to this transaction shall be construed to be part of this transaction unless incorporated in writing herein.

8) We do hereby agree to carry out and fulfill the terms and conditions as specified herein. If either party fails to do so, he or she agrees to pay the expenses of enforcing this agreement, including reasonable attorney fees.

9) Buyer and Seller agree that notice will be given to the Broker if any changes are made to this agreement.

By: ______________________________ agent/broker.

I agree to purchase the above described property on the terms and conditions herein stated:

______________________________ (Buyer)
______________________________ (Buyer)
Executed this ____ day of ________, 19____.

Seller

I agree to sell the above described property on the terms and conditions herein stated, and agree to pay the above signed broker as commission ____________ or one half of the deposit should same be forfeited by purchaser, provided said amount shall not exceed the full amount of said commission.

______________________________ (Seller)
______________________________ (Seller)
Executed this ____ day of ________, 19____.
at ____ A.M./P.M.

7

The Money Maker: Lease-Option

Various opportunities are available to you for investing in real estate. Once you have digested the information available, you can direct your energy to the investment concept that best suits your needs and long-term goals. Keep in mind that real estate essentially is a long-term investment. Granted, big money can be made in short-term speculation, but in order to get the most for your investment you must look at your real estate holdings as a long-term investment. As long as you're patient and use the various methods in this and the next chapter, your chances of success at investing are extremely high.

THE LEASE-OPTION CONCEPT

An option to purchase is a contract by which the owner of a property (optionor) gives the right to purchase the property to another party (optionee). The optionee, or holder of the option, must purchase at a specified price within a set period of time and pay an option fee (consideration).

A lease with option to purchase, or lease-option, is a lease in which the tenant has a leasehold interest in the property along with an option to purchase it.

The lease-option concept is not entirely new. Owners of real property have been offering options for eons, however they have been primarily used on undeveloped land and sophisticated commercial real estate packages. The use of lease-options on residential real estate is relatively new and gained popularity when interest rates began to soar in the late 1970s. By 1981 mortgage interest rates had peaked at 17 percent, the real estate market was in shock, and nobody was buying because no one could afford to. Because interest rates were so high, seasoned VA and FHA loans that carried low interest rates became very valuable.

During this period I had purchased several homes and assumed these low-interest-rate government loans. In doing so, I discovered that instead of merely renting to tenants, I could also offer them an option to purchase and collect a handsome option fee every month. With the tenant paying me a monthly opt fee of $150 or more, my monthly cash flow increased instantly. I discovered further benefits when I realized that when the option is exercised, no sales commission has to be paid.

As time went by, I found my lease-option tenants take better care of the property than tenants who are simply renting with no option to purchase. One of the greatest advantages of the lease option is that, should the tenant fail to exercise the option within the time limit of the agreement, the tenant forfeits all option fees.

The true value of the low-interest-rate and assumable-loan properties I had purchased began to blossom. I found that I could take a 7 percent first mortgage and a 10 percent second mortgage, wrap them in an all-inclusive mortgage at a rate of 12 percent, and offer this new financing to my tenant along with an option to purchase at a specific sales price. This total creation of new financing offers you, the optionor, tremendous profits over the term of the agreement.

A LEASE-OPTION EXAMPLE

I lease-optioned this property three years ago.

Purchase price	$37,000
Down payment	4,500
Cost to fix up	1,500

The balance owing was a first loan of $15,000 at 7 percent and a second of $17,300 payable at 10 percent interest only with the balance payable in 7 years. Total monthly payments on both loans, including taxes and insurance, were $297 per month.

After fixing up the property at a cost of $1,500, I rented it out for $400 with an option to purchase at $49,000. The tenant was to pay me a $150 per month option fee along with $400 rent, or a total of $550 per month. When the tenant exercised his option, I was to receive a $1,320 down payment, and the balance of $46,000 would be payable at 12 percent for a term of 20 years.

Down payment	$4,500	
Cost to fix up	1,500	
Total investment	$6,000	
Income		
Rent	$400	
Option fee	150	
Total monthly gross income	$550	
Total annual gross income		$6,600
Expenses		
First loan, taxes, and insurance	$150	
Second loan	147	
Total monthly expense	$297	
Total annual expense		$3,564
Annual income before income taxes		$3,036
Plus: Equity buildup ($34 × 12)		408
		$3,444

This return on investment of 57.4 percent is a great figure for an investor, but it does not represent the total picture of this particular deal. It represents only cash flow and equity buildup during the option period. Once the tenant exercises the option, the following occurs: Over the year of the option, the tenant has paid $150 × 12 in option fees, or a sum of $1,800. To exercise the option, the tenant must pay an additional $1,200, for a total down payment of $3,000. Since the agreed-upon purchase price is $49,000, the balance remaining to be financed is $46,000 at 12 percent for 20 years.

The following numerical illustration will allow you to understand the lease-option agreement more clearly. As the seller, you wrap the existing financing in an all-inclusive mortgage at a higher rate of interest. For example, I purchased this home for $37,000 with $4,500 down, assuming a first loan of $15,000 at 7 percent and creating a second loan for the balance of $17,500. I spent $1,500 fixing it up, then lease-optioned it for $49,000 at 12 percent with $3,000 down.

Purchased at $37,000

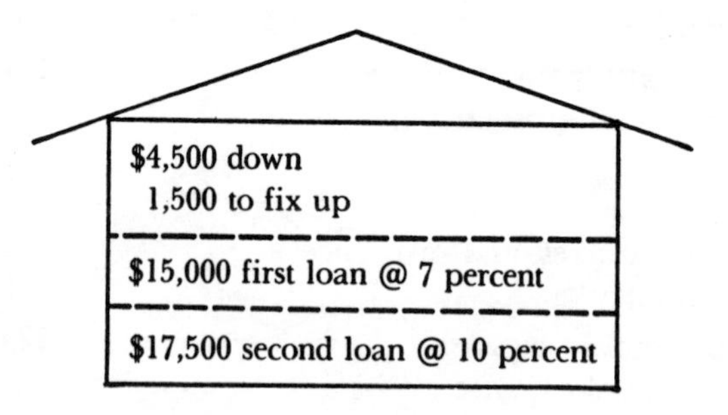

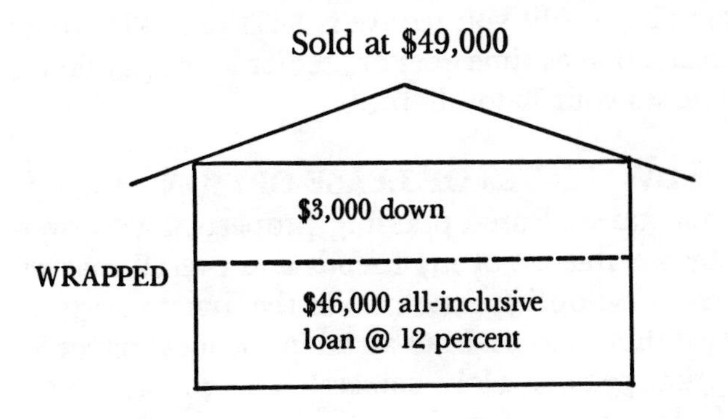

Here's what occurs before the tenant exercises the option:

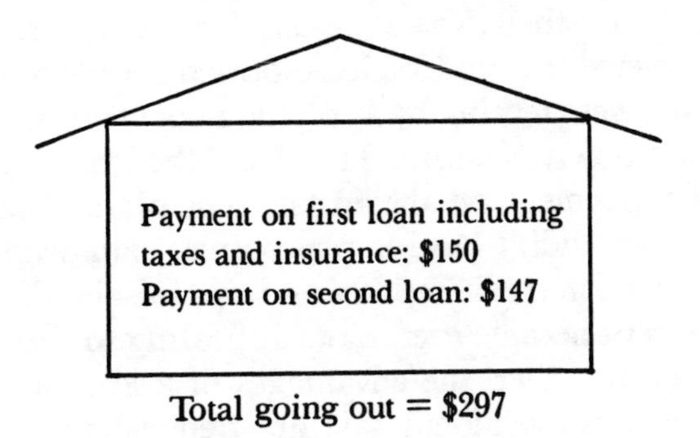

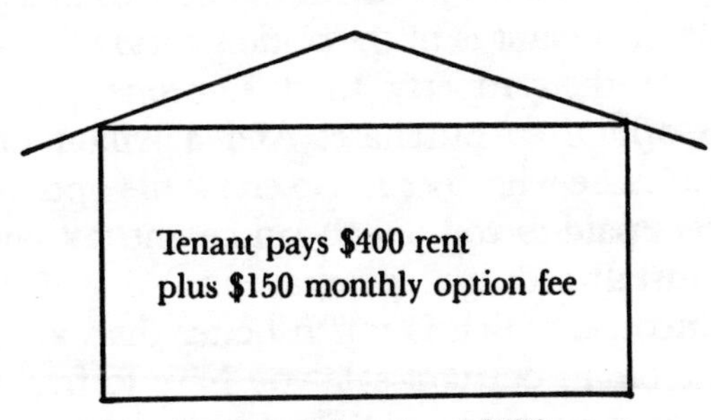

Total monthly profit you receive is $253 plus $34 equity buildup. Note, that as time goes on, senior loans pay down, which increases your monthly profit.

ADVANTAGES OF LEASE-OPTION

When I first started lease-optioning property, I was overwhelmed by the interest of my friends and overall marketability of the lease-option concept. For the first property on which I tried this concept, I ran an ad in the local paper for a lease-option tenant. Holy smokes! The phone started ringing off the hook. Before the lease-option advertisement, I ran an ad on the same property, but only for a rental tenant without the option to purchase, and I only received a couple of calls a day. But under the lease-option ad I received over 15 calls a day. Then I started analyzing the situation to try to understand why there was so much demand for my property. I discovered that under a lease-option people could buy a home they were renting by applying a monthly option fee toward their down payment. They liked the idea of making their down payment on the installment plan. Once they found out they didn't have to pay points, loan origination fees, and fees for credit reports and appraisals, the lease-option concept became even more appealing to them.

To me as the seller, the advantages of a lease-option as opposed to a conventional sale are tremendous. Just for starters, I won't have to pay a sales commission, and on a $60,000 sale that's $3,600 in savings. The second advantage is that while the tenant is in the option period, he will take better care of the property than someone just renting without an option to purchase. And a tenant under an option to purchase who does not exercise the option forfeits all option fees paid to you. Furthermore, the tax savings by selling on installment are advantageous. You also receive long-term income, which is much better than an outright sale, because on an outright sale you have to find another investment for your proceeds. The final advantage is that you profit from existing low-interest-rate loans because when you sell, the existing loans are wrapped at a higher rate of interest.

HOW TO DO IT

Finding Your Lease-Option Tenant

The following is a sample advertisement that I ran in my local newspaper when I was searching for a lease-option tenant:

> Rent with OPTION TO BUY: 3 br, 2.5 ba, beautiful custom home on .5 acres, horse zoned near Warm Springs and Valley View, fireplace, country kitchen with all appliances, hardwood floors, great view of strip, fenced and landscaped, fruit trees and covered patio. $900. Call 555-3953.

When you compose your advertisement, feature the option to buy. It is your greatest selling feature and will attract the most prospects.

Determining the Interest Rate to Charge

What interest rate should you charge on the all-inclusive loan you will carry? As a general rule of thumb, I would charge just a little less than what conventional lenders are charging for first mortgages. If conventional lenders are making loans at 11 percent, then charge 10.5 percent. The reason you want to charge a little less is that you are actually competing with other lenders, and it just makes good business sense to be fair and reasonable with your buyers. Be sure to let your buyers know what a good deal they're getting. Remind them that conventional lenders charge points and fees for originating loans, which they won't have to pay under your all-inclusive loan.

You will need to buy a payment table for monthly mortgage loans in order to determine the correct monthly payment for a specific interest rate. Contemporary Books and Financial Publishing make them available through most bookstores.

An Important Note

Under a lease-option agreement it is important that you make the lease a month-to-month agreement instead of a fixed term of one year or more. The reason this is so important is that your tenant could decide not to exercise the option, and in doing so would cease making option payments to you. If you and the tenant were under a long-term lease agreement and the tenant decided not to exercise the option, he would still have the right to occupy the premises under the terms of the lease. However, if you were bound to a month-to-month agreement, the tenant could be moved out in 30 days and a new lease-option tenant could be substituted.

Sample Agreement

Shown on the next page is a sample form of a lease-option agreement.

THE LEASE-OPTION FORTUNE MAKER

You really have to experience the feeling of having a great money-maker (it's an even better feeling to have 20 or more) that keeps paying off month after month, year after year. Here's a property that you personally bought and fixed up with your own bare hands, and now it's out there in the midst of the city, paying you a handsome income. I really didn't appreciate it myself until my third fixer-upper was purchased and lease-optioned.

When I first started in this business, I really didn't get the most for my money (sometimes I lost money), and I really didn't have much control while renting. When a property was sold, I was totally cashed out, and it usually took me quite a while to find another property to invest the proceeds in. Probably like you, I worked at a full-time job, and to find another good investment wasn't easy, because I just didn't have the time. I had a lot of management problems too, but I learned how to remedy those problems over the years. Under the lease-option concept, you do not have these

Option to Purchase

This option is made and entered into this _____ day of 19___ by and between ________________________, hereinafter called Optionor (owner), and ________________________, hereinafter called Optionee. Subject property is a single-family residence located at ________________________________. Optionor hereby agrees to grant an option to purchase to Optionee based on the following terms and conditions:

Provided that Optionee shall not then be in default of leased property, Optionee to have option to purchase subject property at a price of $__________ for one year beginning ________________________. 19___, and expiring ____, 19___.

Optionee agrees to pay a monthly option fee of $__________ beginning ________________________, 19___, to Optionor, which will be applied toward the purchase price. Optionee further agrees to pay a down payment of $__________ to exercise this option. [Note: Down payment could be an amount less all option fees already paid to Optionor.]

Optionee agrees to finance the balance owing of $__________ secured by an all-inclusive deed of trust [or mortgage] in favor of Optionor at _____% per annum for 20 years at $__________ per month.

Optionor agrees to apply all security deposits and cleaning fees under lease agreement toward down payment upon execution of this option.

Optionee agrees to purchase subject property in an as-is condition.

The parties hereto have executed this option on this date first above written.

Optionor	Optionee
By:________________________	By:________________________

problems because you maintain control of the property over the long term and it continually brings in steady profits, as opposed to one big profit then a search for another.

Here's how the lease-option fortune maker works:

Step 1

You start with an initial cash base of $4,500, with which you buy a house with a $3,000 down payment and fix it up for $1,500. This is all the money you will ever need. All additional investments will be paid for from income created from the property. Now you move in your lease-option tenant. He pays you $400 per month in rent and an option fee of $150 per month for 12 months, plus a $500 security deposit.

During the option period, you take in $550 (rent plus option fee) and pay out $300 per month, realizing $250 per month positive cash flow. At the end of the option period (one year), your profit is $3,000 ($250 × 12).

To exercise the option, the tenant is obligated to pay you a down payment of $1,200. You now have a $3,000 profit and $1,200 down payment, plus a $500 security deposit for a total of $4,700. Results: You now have $4,500 in cash with change left over to make another investment.

You pay out $300 per month

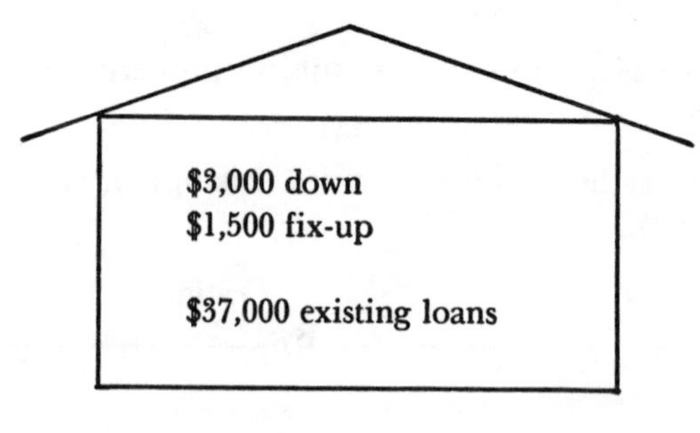

$41,500 total cost

You take in $550 per month

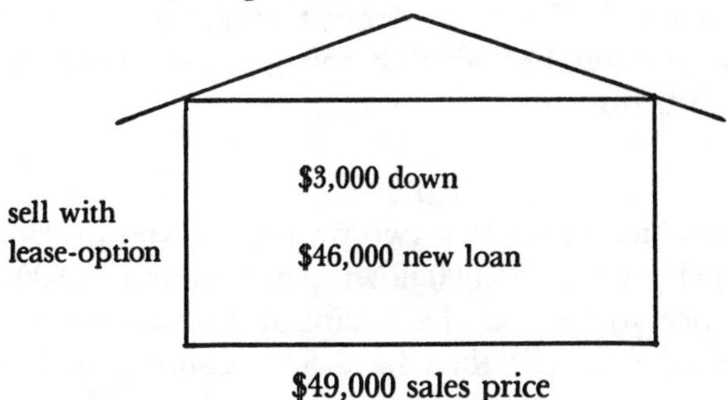

Note: This lease-option agreement is structured in such a way that once the tenant exercises the option, the payments to the seller stay the same. Although the tenant no longer pays an option fee, he now makes payments to the seller on a new all-inclusive loan.

Step 2

Now the $4,500 in cash you earned from the first property can be invested in a second property. As with the first property, you invest $3,000 in a down payment and $1,500 fixing it up.

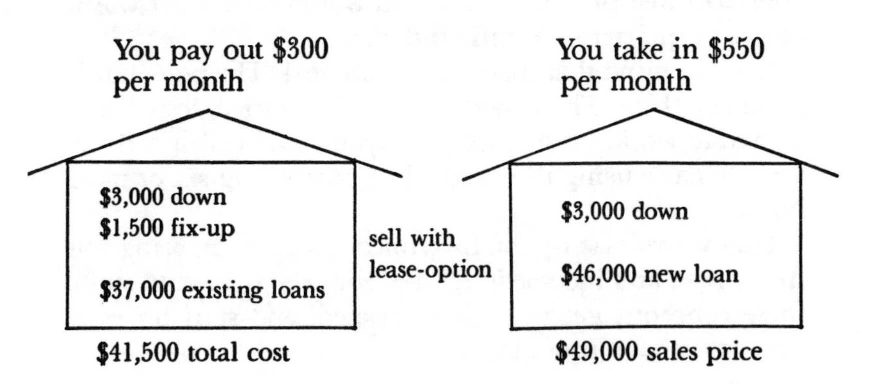

Once you've found a tenant to lease-option the property, you will have $250 per month coming in from each of two properties, or a total of $500 per month positive cash flow. You receive a new $500 security deposit, and in eight months you have an additional $4,000 (8 × $500), or a total of $4,500 to invest in a third property.

Step 3

As in the purchase of the first two properties, you invest in a third property with a $3,000 down payment and $1,500 to fix it up. Once you've found a tenant to lease-option your third property, you will then have $250 coming in from each property, or a total of $750 per month positive cash flow. In 6 months you have an additional $4,500 (6 × $750) to invest in a fourth property.

Further Growth

In the next steps, you continue as you did in step 3 every time you accumulate enough cash to buy and fix up more properties.

After a few years of using this method, the results will be astounding. Let's just suppose you could buy and lease-option six houses a year. It would mean that after three years your yearly net income would exceed $54,000 from your acquired properties, and you would have a net worth of over a quarter of a million dollars.

Keep in mind that these figures are real. The potential is definitely there. These methods have been tried, tested, and proved to work. Within six years, you could realistically be a millionaire using this method of purchasing six or more houses a year.

I know the lease-option investment concept can bring you the growth and income it did me. You merely have to study these concepts, get yourself motivated, and start on your own investment program.

8

More Money-Making Concepts

THE PASADENA CONCEPT

Pasadena is a lovely, mature city in southern California, considered a suburb of Los Angeles. It has many older homes built with rock foundations that have deteriorated over the years due to age and earthquakes. Neither local lenders nor the FHA would originate new loans on these homes. Further complicating matters, most of these homes were poorly located in slum neighborhoods. With no financing available, many of these rock-foundation homes eventually were foreclosed on by the original lien holders.

A lender who takes back a property through foreclosure typically removes any occupants, boards up windows and doors to secure the property, and eventually sells it. These boarded-up properties often sit on the market for years, until the lender eventually concedes to an extremely low cash price from an innovative speculator.

At one time I lived in Los Angeles and had the opportunity to team up with a house-moving contractor with the intention of investing in these homes. Back then we could buy one of these rock-foundation foreclosures for $5,000 to

$8,000 cash. Keep in mind that one of these Pasadena board-ups had been sitting in a crummy neighborhood unattended for who knows how many years. Many were bathed in local gang grafitti with most of the plumbing ripped from the fittings. It was no pretty picture, and to invest here meant plenty of hard work.

The secret to the Pasadena concept was to raise the house off its foundation, knock out the existing foundation and pour a new one, then set the house back down on its new foundation. Once the house was sitting on its new foundation, we proceeded to fix it up and sell it. Because we no longer had a rock foundation, the FHA and conventional lenders would now lend on the property.

On one particular property the foundation work, including raising and lowering the house, cost about $5,000. Fixing it up for resale cost another $6,000. So now we had a total of $16,000 in the property, including the $5,000 cash purchase price. Six months after purchasing the property, we had it sold for $52,000 with a new FHA loan to finance it. After all costs were considered, we netted a tidy $32,000, which I happily split with my overjoyed and overworked partner. Most of the proceeds were generated from hard work, but the real key to those profits was innovation. Who would ever have thought to simply lift the house up and pour a new foundation?

SHORT-TERM ROLLOVER 100 PERCENT FINANCED

This investment concept requires finding a lender who will loan you the entire proceeds for a short term. First you find the property and your lender finances it. Once you have purchased it, fix it up and resell. Then you pay off your lender, and you earn the proceeds.

The key here, as in most real estate transactions, is to find the financing. Typically you will need a mortgage banker, one who represents investors with $50,000 to $100,000 to invest for a nine-month term.

Before you go ahead and locate a property, it is necessary to already have a lender tentatively set up for such a transaction. Then, once a property is located, you would make an offer contingent upon your acquiring sufficient financing. If the offer is accepted, your proposal would then be considered by the lender. If by chance your lender will not lend you the proceeds, your offer would then be voided because of the financing contingency inserted into your offer.

The cost for such a loan in today's market would be 14 percent interest and 4 points ($2,000 on a $50,000 loan). The investor earns the 14 percent, and the loan broker earns the points.

You can use this rule of thumb: if you can purchase a home at no more than two-thirds of its market value after it's fixed up, you can make a good deal. For example, if you could sell a home for $100,000 in good condition, then you should pay no more than two-thirds of that, or approximately $67,000.

Let's detail this method to see how it works. To begin with, you need a lender who will advance the entire proceeds, including fix-up capital. You use the loan proceeds to pay all existing loans in full and to pay the seller in cash for his equity. The lender will then create a new first mortgage on the subject property. With the fix-up capital from the new mortgage, refurbish the property and then resell at a substantial profit. When the property is sold, you pay off the lender entirely with a new first loan (either conventional or VA/FHA), and you earn the differential, which is the profit.

Ideally, buying a property at substantially below market value works best when the seller has a large equity position in the property and is unwilling to carry back a note for his equity and the property requires much repair. In this case, the seller will be more inclined to reduce the selling price substantially in order to be totally cashed out of the property.

Here's how the numbers work: assume you find a home that, after careful analysis, you determine you can sell for $100,000 after investing $5,000 to fix it up. Using two-thirds of market value, you determine that if you can buy this home for up to $67,000 you can earn a sizable profit.

Purchase price	$67,000
Closing costs	500
Cost to fix up	5,000
Finance cost (4 points plus 14 percent for 6 months) [represents 4 points on $72,000 plus 14% interest]	7,920
Taxes and insurance for 6 months	350
Utilities	200
Total cost before sale	$80,970

Selling price	$100,000
Less: Closing costs	500
Less: Sales commission (6 percent)	6,000
Less: Total costs before sale	80,970
Net profit	$12,530

These calculations include a 6 percent sales commission, which is optional. I would suggest using the services of a Realtor, because it is necessary in a transaction of this type to procure a quick sale, due to the nine-month time limitation on the loan. Furthermore, when you buy a property and intend to resell it within a year, most title companies will allow you to pay an additional retainer (usually $50), which will be the total cost of title insurance required when you sell. The cost of such a policy to the seller is usually about $500, so you can save $450 by paying in advance for the title insurance retainer.

CONVERSIONS

If you have lived in a particular area for some time, you have probably noticed that over time older buildings are now functioning in a completely different capacity than that for which they were originally designed. Rental apartment buildings are now condominiums. Old homes have become office buildings. Gas stations have become retail outlets. Prime farm acreage is now residential housing tracts or an industrial complex.

These conversions occur for two main reasons: changes in demand and changes in competition. A city's outward growth causes the demand for usable land to increase. For example, a once productive farm located on the outskirts of a growing metropolis is no longer able to turn a profit on its crops. So the farmer sells to a developer who converts the land to a large housing tract or a shopping mall. In addition, competition may make a former use of the property unprofitable. For example, there may be so much nearby competition that a building that was once a thriving gas station is now a retail outlet.

For the creative investor, conversions provide boundless opportunities. Many years ago I worked for a shrewd real estate developer who would buy single-family residences on strategic corner locations. His intention was to keep the house rented until he could eventually convert it into a more profitable rental use, such as a commercial office building or a valuable retail outlet. He maintained an advantage by purchasing strategically located land with a rental house on it, as opposed to vacant land. This way he could receive some income from the house, instead of maintaining a vacant parcel until it was time to convert.

Relative Values

Let's compare relative values of a typical 20-acre parcel of land used for different purposes. Raw land used for cattle grazing would be least valuable at approximately $1,000 per acre. If the same land were converted to a subdivision in which a developer could build a tract of homes with five lots to an acre, then the land could sell for about $25,000 an acre. The highest value of this parcel would come from using the land for commercial office buildings or a shopping center; then it would sell for about $200,000 an acre.

As you can see, changing the use is like turning silver into gold. But how can you take advantage of these changes in land use? You can start by obtaining an overall zoning map from your city's planning department. Each area within the city limits has a particular zoning (agricultural, residential, multi-unit, commercial, and industrial). Of course the property you wish to convert must be within the area of the higher-use zoning (multi-unit residential located inside a commercial zone). Otherwise, you will have to apply for a zoning change, which requires a change in the zoning law. To change most zoning laws requires much time and effort. If you are interested in pursuing this matter any further, check with your local city planning department and inquire into the necessary procedure.

Condominium Conversion

To convert a multi-unit apartment building into individual condominium units, you want a situation where you can purchase rental units inexpensively enough so that each will easily and inexpensively convert to a salable condo. This means you should buy at $20,000 per unit or less and sell for $35,000 per unit or more. For example, if you purchase a 10-unit rental for $200,000 ($20,000 per unit) and convert to 10 individual condo units, selling each at $35,000 per unit, you will make a $15,000 profit on each unit before conversion costs.

You must also consider the legal procedures necessary to accomplish condo conversion. First, the city has to approve the change in use. You must submit plans explaining exactly how you intend to make your conversion. If the city considers your plans adequate, it will approve your conversion. If not, you will have to make certain changes (additional parking, more bathrooms, etc.) before you get permission to convert.

Before going ahead with plans for a condo conversion, analyze the local area to determine what comparable condos are selling for. If you can purchase rental units at a low enough price, sell the converted units, and earn a tidy profit while absorbing time and cost to convert, then by all means go ahead with your plans.

Converting Apartments to an Office Complex

Typically, office space rents for at least twice as much as apartment living space. Based on that observation alone, it appears highly profitable to convert. But before you go ahead, you should consider some important questions:

- Is the property you wish to convert within a commercial zone? If not, can it easily be changed to the proper zoning?
- What is the current vacancy rate for office space in the area of the subject property? If too much space is already available, it would be unwise to convert.
- Do you have adequate parking for office space? Typically, the city will require one parking space for every 500 square feet of rentable office space.
- How much will it cost to convert? Would a bank lend you the money to finance the cost of conversion?

Study the situation carefully. Thoroughly analyze the finances of your projected conversion. Keeping in tune with the requirements given, if you can convert and finance at a reasonable cost, and still earn a profit, then go ahead with your plans. Remember the one-for-two rule: each dollar of fix-up cost should equal at least two dollars of increased value.

RENTING

Renting your property is an alternative you might consider to receive income, tax shelter, and eventual appreciation from your investment property. This investment concept is similar to a lease-option, except no option to buy would be attached to the rental agreement, and no option fee would be paid to you.

A rental property can be a worthwhile investment even if the numbers show a less than break-even condition (monthly rent equals, or is less than, principal and interest and normal expenses). For instance, you rent a property for $500 a month while your expenses and debt service are $500 a month. You show zero net income, but due to appreciation and tax benefits from owning rental property, this property can still be considered a good investment. Because of depreciation, you could actually show a loss of about $6,000 on a $60,000 property during the first year for income-tax purposes. If you were in the 30 percent tax bracket, that would be $1,800 that could be deducted from your normal wage earnings. Furthermore, consider that the property will appreciate at least 5 percent annually. Equity buildup is an additional big advantage of renting your property.

Negative cash flow or a break-even condition makes good sense when the investment property is located where real estate values are appreciating rapidly. Typically, this would be an area that is in high demand. For example, during the last 10 years along the coast of southern California, property adjacent to the ocean appreciated at a rate in excess of 20 percent a year.

By itself, renting seldom generates enough net income to be a quick money-making concept. The major benefits from renting are tax shelter, equity buildup, and appreciation. Therefore, renting could be recommended as a viable investment method over lease-option only when you can expect more than average appreciation on your investment, or if you simply need the tax shelter to protect other income.

SELLING THE INVESTMENT OUTRIGHT

Selling outright and receiving all the proceeds in cash is another method you might consider. However, this method has many disadvantages. First consider the tax ramifications. Under current tax laws, you must hold a property at least six months before it can qualify for long-term capital gains (one year if acquired before June 23, 1984), and then 40 percent of the gain is still taxable. If the property is held for less than six months, the entire gain is taxable.

The other disadvantage of selling your property outright is that you have to find another investment for the proceeds from the sale. You could put the proceeds into savings, but who wants to earn a meager 5 percent? Realistically, you have to seek out a new real estate money maker in order to gain a substantial return on investment.

About the only real advantage to selling outright is that you'll have plenty of ready cash available. The only time this is really an advantage is when you have another good investment to put the ready cash into.

SELLING TIPS

Let's compare selling on installment (lease-option) with an outright sale that will totally cash you out of the property. Selling on installment has the following advantages:

- Instead of paying capital gains taxes on the entire proceeds all at one time, you pay taxes only on the small portion of the installment proceeds you receive.
- You receive regular income over the long term as your hard-earned money is properly invested with continued equity appreciation as loans pay down.
- Under a lease-option agreement, you have no sales commission to pay.

Under the outright sale, about the only advantage is that you have ready cash available. But let's look at all the disadvantages of an outright sale:

- Probably the most glaring disadvantage is that once you sell the property, you have to find another investment vehicle for the proceeds from the sale. That can cost you plenty of valuable time.

- You have to pay capital gains taxes all in one lump sum, and you have to pay more if you held the property for less than six months.
- An outright sale takes away from property accumulation and makes ready cash available for spending—sometimes frivolous spending. New cars, boats, and vacations are nice . . . but hardly a wise investment for someone who wants to retire by the age of 35.

These are good reasons for *not* selling the property, and these reasons apply most of the time. But sometimes these reasons do not apply, and those are the times when you should sell the property.

For example, you need the cash to better your investment position, so you decide to sell. For any number of reasons you're against taking out a short-term loan or taking on a partner with cash. The property you want is a real bargain, the price is right, the terms are great, but you don't have the down payment.

Here, you might consider selling one of your properties to raise the necessary down payment, especially if you are going to improve your financial condition. Let us assume that you could sell one of your houses in which you have a large equity position. The property you want is a 20-unit apartment building, and the owner wants $30,000 down. You decide that by selling the house and buying the apartment building you will substantially increase your cash flow and have much better leverage. You then have definitely improved your financial condition.

Diminishing Return on Equity Dollars

Deciding whether or not to sell an individual property to buy another is based on how much equity is in the property you want to sell. There are certain considerations concerning time to sell that are based on the mathematics of equity growth. It is important to understand the principles involved. As you will see, there is a point at which equity buildup causes the rate of return on your equity to fall substantially below the rate of return you received during the early years of ownership.

Here is an example of equity buildup in a property of mine, showing the net income per year and the yearly rate of return on invested capital. From this example, you will be able to understand why, at some point determined through calculating your rate of return, it is necessary to sell your property in order to keep earning a high rate of return on your investments.

I purchased an apartment building a few years ago for $110,000, with a $9,000 down payment, and $3,000 invested in fixing it up. Thus, my first year's equity position, before appreciation, was $12,000. After a year, when all improvements were completed and rent increased, the fair market value of the property was $135,000. So, in the second year of ownership, my new equity position equaled the initial investment of $12,000, plus the increase in property value of $25,000, or $37,000.

Please refer to the following calculations to see how this increase in equity affected my rate of return on this investment:

First Year of Ownership

Initial cost of property	$110,000
Down payment	9,000
Cost to fix up	3,000
Total investment, or first-year equity	$12,000

First-year net income	$5,400

The return on equity in the first year is:

$5,400 ÷ $12,000 = 45 percent

Second Year of Ownership

Fair market value, second year	$135,000
Less: Initial cost of property	110,000
Gain in value, or equity	25,000
Plus: Initial investment	12,000
Total second-year equity	$37,000
Second-year net income	$5,400

In the above example, note the diminishing rate of return on my equity from the first year to the second. The reason for this reduction is that my $25,000 profit, derived from improvements and appreciation, has not been reinvested. It is just sitting there. This $25,000 is only on paper. It is not "real" until I convert it to dollars and cents by using it, which I can do by selling the property (in which case the $25,000 will be in my pocket and I can reinvest it), or trading up.

When you are deciding when to sell a specific property, you must consider diminishing returns on equity. It is often wise, once you've derived a substantial profit from a property, to sell or exchange it, to avoid the equity buildup that so dramatically reduces returns.

Tax-Deferred Exchanges

There's another method you should consider when you decide to sell and reinvest in another property—a tax-deferred exchange. Should you decide to sell your property, you will have to pay capital gains tax on the profit. If you exchange your property, you defer the capital gains tax as long as:

1. The property you exchange for is of equal or greater value;
2. There is no mortgage relief (the mortgage you assume is equal to or greater than the mortgage you are trading out of); and

3. You pay tax on any consideration (cash or any other non–real estate) you receive along with the property in exchange.

Guidelines If You Do Decide to Sell

1. When you're in the process of buying and you're negotiating the second or third loan the seller will carry, you obviously do not want a due-on-sale clause in the note, because it will severely inhibit your ability to resell the property. In contrast, when you sell the property, the opposite is true; you need the due-on-sale clause to protect you if the property is sold again before you are paid for it. The due-on-sale clause states that all your remaining equity in the note is due and payable in full if the buyer subsequently sells the property. At a later time you may choose to ignore the due-on-sale clause, but never limit your options by omitting it from your agreement.
2. If the overall demand for real estate is strong (a seller's market), try to sell the property yourself, without a real estate broker, and save the commission. If you do decide to list with a Realtor, use a well-established, reputable firm that can get the job done. Before you sign the listing agreement, be sure the term of the listing agreement is not too long, which would hamper your flexibility. A 60- to 90-day listing is adequate, although your real estate agent would argue differently.
3. Know exactly what you want out of the property in price and terms. If your price and terms are fair and reasonable, you will sell more quickly. If your price is excessive and your terms unreasonable, it is unlikely you will receive any offers at all.
4. Eliminate any uncertainties about the property. Uncertainties make potential buyers uneasy. They include a ragged, dirty carpet or an inoperable heating system.

These things leave prospective buyers with too many questions to answer (how will we fix it and how much will it cost?). It is likely that prospective buyers would rather look elsewhere than buy a property full of uncertainties. Besides, you're in the business of buying, fixing up, and reselling. You don't sell fixer-uppers, you buy them . . . and then fix them up. You should not be selling a home in disrepair.

5. Prequalify prospective buyers. When I first started in this business and began receiving calls from prospective buyers, I would get real excited. I would drop everything to go show the house. Then the prospects didn't show up, or the house was too small, or they wanted a fenced yard and a pool. I could have just taken the time to prequalify over the phone. All it takes is a few questions, and you can save plenty of time, gas, and frustration. Get as much information as you can over the phone. Find out exactly what the prospect is looking for. Maybe this particular home won't do, but you might have another that will suit his needs.
6. Explain all financing terms in black and white so they are recognizable. Figures on paper eliminate uncertainties and errors.
7. Finally, be firm and explain everything without leaving any loose ends. Being wishy-washy will only make your prospects uneasy. If a prospect has any questions, be sure to answer them properly. If the buyer has any doubts whatsoever, he most likely will not buy.

9

Property Management: One Man's Dilemma Is Another Man's Profit

(Note: For a more thorough analysis of property management, please refer to my book, *How to Manage Real Estate Profitably*, published by Contemporary Books.)

FURNISHED OR UNFURNISHED?

Supplying furniture (beds, couches, and tables) should be avoided. The main reason is less turnover. When a family has to move all its own furniture into your available unit, it will make them think twice before moving again. If they didn't have any furniture to move, relocating the entire family could be done in the blink of an eye. Besides, if you supply furniture, then it's your responsibility to maintain it. In the long run, unfurnished rental units produce less turnover than furnished units.

The one exception would be if you owned an apartment building with single-room and studio units. Then furniture would be an asset to the property because studio apartments thrive on active, transient tenants who require furniture. In this case, the amount of rent you charge and security deposit you require should reflect the amount of furniture you supply. Therefore, if you do supply furniture, you can probably be justified in charging $50 to $75 more per month in rent and $250 more in security deposit.

With regard to appliances (washer-dryer, refrigerator), try to avoid supplying them to your tenants. Keep in mind that anything mechanical, like a washer or dryer, will inevitably need repair. And if you own it and do not make some sort of arrangement with your tenant, you are responsible for repair when something goes wrong.

REPAIR WORK

The nitty-gritty of property management and the source of the biggest hassle most landlords face almost daily is the tenant phone call requesting repair work. In the last three years, I have virtually eradicated this hassle in the management of my personal properties simply by making the tenant responsible for the first $100 in repair of the rented property, including appliances. I have inserted in the lease agreement a clause that makes the tenant responsible for the first $100 in repair and maintenance to the property; I am responsible for anything in excess of $100. You might get some static from some tenants when it comes time to sign the lease. If they do quibble about this clause, inform them that you left the washer and dryer on the property as a convenience. You do not want to be responsible for the repair of appliances and will gladly remove them if they are an inconvenience to the tenants.

If you own multi-unit buildings, then most likely you will have to supply washers and dryers. In this case, a washer and dryer room would be required, and you would have the option of having a service company handle the whole washer-dryer operation. Or, if you have plenty of ready cash, you could invest in the coin-operated washer and dryer business.

ADVERTISING

The best way to bring prospects to your door is to use vacancy signs and classified ads in your local newspaper. Vacancy signs must be precise and to the point, qualifying the prospective tenant to a certain degree. For example, your sign might say:

> Rent with Option to Buy, 2-bedroom, call 555-1212.

Stating certain facts about the available unit will eliminate a lot of unqualified prospects who are looking for something you don't have available.

Vacancy signs should be legible and large enough to be easily seen from a passing car. Place signs where they get maximum exposure—either on the side of your building or posted on the lawn near the busiest street.

Classified advertising should also be precise and qualifying in order to eliminate unnecessary calls from unqualified prospects. Start your ad with location, then the type of unit, something like this:

> Spring Mountain & Jones, 3-bedroom, 2-bath. . . .

This way, people looking for a rental are somewhat qualified right at the start of the ad. Anyone looking for a three-bedroom in my locale will call; anyone looking for a two-bedroom is unqualified and will look elsewhere.

After the full description of the available unit, close the ad with the amount of rent you're charging and a phone number to call. The amount of rent is important because you again qualify the prospect. If you're charging more than the prospect can pay, he won't call.

Here's a sample advertisement that proved very effective. It ran in my local newspaper under the section Unfurnished Homes for Rent.

> Rent with Option to Buy—Spring Mountain & Jones, 3br, 2ba, neat and clean, beautifully landscaped & decorated. $560. Call 555-1212.

SHOWING THE UNIT

When you have an ad running in the local newspaper and signs strategically located on the property, the unit has to be ready for showing. Get in the habit of having your available units spick and span throughout. Nothing turns off a good tenant more than a dumpy, dirty place.

Point out the features of the unit and avoid bringing up anything that might be negative about the property. Should the unit have something about it that you feel is a disadvantage, don't bring it up in the conversation. What may be a negative aspect to some, may not be to others. In other words, let the sleeping gremlins rest. Of course, if the tenant brings up a subject, you must be truthful.

RENTING THE UNIT

At this point your prospect has seen the entire premises and has decided to rent it. What do you do now? Get a large deposit; the more you can get, the better off you'll be. Keep in mind that you will be taking the unit off the market now that your prospect has made a deposit, but he hasn't moved in yet or signed anything. If you receive only $25 or $50 to hold the unit, it would be easy for the tenant to skip. But, if he has $300 or more holding the unit, then it would be difficult to back out of the deal.

After you receive an adequate deposit, have your prospective tenant fill out the rental application. A sample form is shown on the next page. The rental application will give you enough information to qualify the tenant. Before you hand over the keys and give possession, be sure that all monies owed to you have been paid in advance. This includes the first month's rent, the security deposit, and the cleaning fee.

Instead of renting to a family, consider renting to three or four single people. Often you can get more monthly rent by renting to singles than to one family. For example, you have a large four-bedroom house available to rent. If one family were to rent the home, you could probably get about $500 to

Rental Application Form

Last name ______________________
First ____
Middle initial ______________________
Spouse's full name ________________________________
Unit to be occupied by _________ adults and _________ children
Present address ________________________________
City ____
State ______________________ Zip _________
How long _____ mos. _____ yrs.
Applicant's birthdate ______________ Driver's license no. __________________________
Social Security No. ______________
Spouse's birthdate ______________ Spouse's driver's license no. __________________________
Spouse's Social Security No. ______________
Present landlord ______________ Phone _________
Monthly payment _________
Employer ______________________ How long on the job __________________________
Employer address ________________________________
Position __________________________ Salary _________
Closest relative ______________
Address ____
City ______________ State ______________ Phone _________
Credit reference ______________________ Account no. __________________________
Credit reference ______________________ Account no. __________________________
Vehicle no. 1 ______________________ License no. __________________________
Vehicle no. 2 ______________________ License no. __________________________
Name of referring party ______________________
Signature of applicant ________________________________
Date ________________

$550 in monthly rent. But if you rented the same home to four singles, you could get $150 to $175 per person in rent, or a total of $600 to $700 per month. Renting to singles would be most practical if your rental property were located near a college. Then you'd have no problem keeping the place rented.

There are certain considerations in renting to several singles. One is the disadvantage of more turnover, as single people move more than families. Furthermore, you should require more in security deposits from single people, as they tend to have more parties and do more damage to the premises than married folks.

QUALIFYING THE TENANT

If a complete stranger approached you on the street and said, "I need your car—may I have your keys?" you would probably tell him, "No." In the home rental business there are many unwise owners who will allow a complete stranger to move into their home because this stranger says, in effect, "I need the use of this $50,000 investment"—your home. This person could be the same stranger who asked for your car. You need information on him before you can do business.

Whether or not your tenant decides to pay rent in the future, he has gained the right to use and enjoy your property and the right of privacy. Should your new tenant fail to pay rent and you wish him removed from the premises, you must do it by "due process of law." In California, this is an unlawful detainer action. In most other states, it is an eviction suit. These actions, if successful, will bring only a judgment for rent monies, court costs, and moving fees. Cases that go to court will undoubtedly require 20 to 30 days or more to remedy. The costs involved, plus additional loss of rent, can get completely out of hand when a professional deadbeat decides to slither onto your premises.

The only way to avoid the professional deadbeat is to

properly check prospective tenants' backgrounds. Telephone a local credit agency and find out what they require to do a credit check for you.

Observation of Human Nature

Here is an observation of human nature that may help future landlords: People who take good care of their vehicle will, in most cases, take good care of the home they live in. Conversely, people who drive a dirty, ill-maintained car in almost every case live dirty and won't take very good care of your property. So, when your prospects drive up to see your available unit, check out what kind of care has been given to the family car. Later, if you have any doubts about whether to rent to them or not, let the condition of the family car help you in making your decision.

Financial Qualification

To qualify the tenant's ability to pay for the rental of your home, follow these guidelines: The rent should not exceed 25 percent of the tenant's total gross income. A tenant with no consumer debt (car loans, credit card payments) can afford to pay one-third of his gross income for rent, but not more. For example, if your prospective tenant grosses $2,000 per month and has a few outstanding debts, then his rent should not exceed $500 (25 percent of $2,000). If your prospect has no installment debt, then he could afford one-third of $2,000, or $667 per month in rent.

Qualifying the Lease-Option Prospect

You'll want to find out two things about your prospective lease-option tenant:

1. Can he afford to buy your house?
2. How is his credit?

These two items are critical to the long-term success of your lease-option agreement. If tenants can't afford to buy or have a poor credit history, then you shouldn't enter into an agreement with them. The headache of late payments or no payments at all, with the likelihood of foreclosure, is a situation you definitely want to avoid.

Begin by having your prospective lease-option tenants fill out a rental application form. Generally speaking, your prospects' total house payment including property taxes and insurance should fall within a range of 25 to 33 percent of their combined gross income. If they don't have much consumer debt (car payments and credit card payments), then their total house payment can be closer to 33 percent of gross income. If they are heavily indebted, then their house payment should not exceed 25 percent of gross income. For example, assume your prospects have a total combined gross income of $2,400 per month with no consumer debt. Then they could afford one-third of $2,400, or $800 per month. If they have some consumer debt, then they can afford 25 percent of $2,400, or $600 per month.

To inquire into your prospects' credit history, call your local TRW Credit Company. They'll inform you of local procedures and what will be required of you.

DEPOSITS

As a general rule of thumb regarding deposits, the more risk to you as the owner, the more you should charge in deposits. A security deposit is a refundable deposit protecting the owner from damage to the premises. Usually, one month's rent is adequate; however, if you rent to a family with children and pets, it would be wise to get at least 25 percent more. Pets and children do cause a little more wear and tear on the property than adults.

Another necessary deposit is the nonrefundable cleaning deposit. This charge normally is in the range of $50 to $100, depending on the size of the rental. Certain states prohibit nonrefundable cleaning fees, in which case you could rename this fee a "one-time leasing charge, nonrefundable."

Be sure you inform your tenant prior to move-in that the security deposit cannot be applied to the last month's rent when he vacates, that it will be held until after the unit is vacated with proper notice and in reasonably good condition.

EVICTION PROCEDURE

The following steps describe a standard eviction procedure:

1. The tenant in default is served with a three-day Notice to Pay Rent or Quit the Premises. The person serving notice should be the marshal, not the landlord or owner, in order to ensure proper legal procedure.
2. An Unlawful Detainer is filed with the municipal court clerk, and a summons is issued.
3. The tenant is served with a summons and complaint.
4. The tenant has the legal right to file against the complaint, pleading his or her case. In that event a trial is held.
5. The default of tenant is taken and given to the owner.
6. The court issues a Writ of Possession.
7. The marshal receives the Writ of Possession.
8. The marshal evicts the tenant.

PREVENTIVE MAINTENANCE TIPS

Besides financial rewards, owning and operating rental property has its headaches and annoyances. However, most of the annoyances can be relieved by doing preventive maintenance and by giving your tenants guidelines to follow.

One of a homeowner's biggest headaches is stopped-up drains. The remedy is to install drain strainers in your bathtubs and bathroom sinks. This inexpensive device traps hair and large material before it can start collecting in your pipes.

The most common cause of bathtub and toilet drains being blocked is children's small toys. If you rent to people with children, tell them the reason for the drain strainer and request that their children not put small toys in bathtubs and toilets. Remember the old saying, "An ounce of prevention is worth a pound of cure."

SAMPLE LEASE

Here is a sample of the contents of a residential lease.

Residential Lease

1. This Lease made this ________ day of ________, 19________ by and between ____________________ ____, hereinafter called Landlord, and ____________________ ____, hereinafter called Tenant.
2. **Description:** Witnesseth, the Landlord, in consideration of the rents to be paid and the covenants and agreements to be performed by the Tenant, does hereby lease unto the Tenant the following described premises located thereon situated in the City of ____________, County of ____________, State of ____________, commonly known as ____.
3. **Terms:** For the term of ____________ (months/years) commencing on ________, 19____, and ending on ________________, 19____.
4. **Rent:** Tenant shall pay Landlord, as rent for said premises, the sum of ________ dollars ($________) per month, payable in advance on the first day of each month during the term hereof at Landlord's address above or said other place as Landlord may hereafter designate in writing. Tenant agrees to pay a $25 late fee if rent is not paid within 5 days of due date.
5. **Security Deposit:** Landlord herewith acknowledges the receipt of ________ dollars ($________), which he is to retain as security for the faithful performance of the provisions of this lease. If Tenant fails to pay rent, or defaults with respect to any provision of this lease,

Landlord may use the security deposit to cure the default or compensate Landlord for all damages sustained by Landlord. Tenant shall immediately on demand reimburse Landlord the sum equal to that portion of security deposit expended by Landlord so as to maintain the security deposit in the sum initially deposited with Landlord. If Tenant performs all obligations under this lease, the security deposit, or that portion thereof that was not previously applied by Landlord, shall be returned to Tenant within 21 days after the expiration of this lease, or after Tenant has vacated the premises.

6. **Possession:** It is understood that if the Tenant shall be unable to enter into and occupy the premises hereby leased at the time above provided, by reason of the said premises not being ready for occupancy, or by reason of holding over of any previous occupant of said premises, the Landlord shall not be liable in damage to the Tenant therefore, but during the period the Tenant shall be unable to occupy said premises as hereinbefore provided, the rental therefore shall be abated and the Landlord is to be the sole judge as to when the premises are ready for occupancy.
7. **Use:** Tenant agrees that said premises during the term of this lease shall be used and occupied by ________ adults and ________ children, and no animals, and for no other purpose whatsoever without the written consent of the Landlord, and that Tenant will not use the premises for any purpose in violation of any law, municipal ordinance or regulation, and that on any breach of this agreement the Landlord may at his option terminate this lease and re-enter and repossess the leased premises.
8. **Utilities:** Tenant will pay for all charges for all water supplied to the premises and shall pay for all gas, heat, electricity, and other services supplied to the premises, except as herein provided.
9. **Repairs and Maintenance:** The Landlord shall at his expense, except for the first $100 in cost which the Tenant pays, keep and maintain the exterior and interior walls, roof, electrical wiring, heating and air-conditioning system,

water heater, built-in appliances, and water lines in good condition and repair, except where damage has been caused by negligence or abuse of the Tenant, in which case Tenant shall repair same at his sole expense.

Tenant hereby agrees that the premises are now in good condition and shall at his sole expense maintain the premises and appurtenances in the manner in which they were received, reasonable wear and tear excepted.

The ______________ agrees to maintain landscaping and swimming pool (if any). Tenant agrees to adequately water landscaping.

10. **Alterations and Additions:** The Tenant shall not make any alterations, additions, or improvements to said premises without the Landlord's written consent. All alterations, additions, or improvements made by either of the parties hereto upon the premises, except movable furniture, shall be the property of the Landlord, and shall remain upon and be surrendered with the premises at the termination of this lease.

11. **Assignment:** The Tenant will not assign or transfer this lease or hypothecate or mortgage the same or sublet said premises without the written consent of the Landlord.

12. **Default:** If the Tenant shall abandon or vacate said premises before the end of the term of this lease, or if default shall be made by the Tenant in the payment of said rent or any part hereof, or if the Tenant shall fail to perform any of the Tenant's agreements in this lease, then and in each and every instance of such abandonment, vacation, or default, the Tenant's right to enter said premises shall be suspended, and the Landlord may at his option enter said premises, change the locks on the doors of said leased premises, and remove and exclude the Tenant from said premises.

13. **Entry by Landlord:** Tenant shall allow the Landlord or his agents to enter the premises at all reasonable times and upon reasonable notice for the purpose of inspecting or maintaining the premises, or to show it to prospective tenants or purchasers.

14. **Attorney's Fees:** The Tenant agrees to pay all costs, expenses, and reasonable attorney's fees including obtaining advice of counsel incurred by Landlord in enforcing by legal action or otherwise any of Landlord's rights under this lease or under any law of this state.

15. **Holding Over:** If Tenant, with the Landlord's consent, remains in possession of the premises after expiration of the term of this lease, such possession will be deemed a month-to-month tenancy at a rental equal to the last monthly rental, and upon all the provisions of this lease applicable to such a month-to-month tenancy.

The parties hereto have executed this lease on the date first above written.

Landlord:	Tenant:
By: ______________________	By: ______________________
By: ______________________	By: ______________________

10

Tax Savings from Depreciation

(**Note**: This chapter is a reprint from the Internal Revenue Service, Publication 17, [Rev. Nov. 85].)

DEPRECIATION

In general, if you buy property to use in a trade or business or to earn rent or royalty income, and the property has a useful life of more than one year, you cannot deduct its entire cost in one year. Instead, you must spread the cost over more than one year and deduct a part of it each year. For most types of property, this is called "depreciation."

The discussion in this chapter gives you basic information on depreciation, including the section 179 deduction and the accelerated cost recovery system (ACRS). Use Form 4562, Depreciation and Amortization to report your depreciation deduction, including the section 179 deduction. If you need more information, see Publication 534, Depreciation.

WHAT CAN BE DEPRECIATED

Many different kinds of property can be depreciated, as for

example, machinery, buildings, vehicles, patents, copyrights, furniture, and equipment.

Property is depreciable if it meets all three of these tests:

1. It must be used in business, or held for the production of income (for example, to earn rent or royalty income).
2. It must have a useful life that can be determined, and its useful life must be longer than one year. The useful life of a piece of property is an estimate of how long you can expect to use it in your business or to earn rent or royalty income.
3. It must be something that wears out, decays, gets used up, becomes obsolete, or loses value from natural causes.

Depreciable property may be tangible or intangible. Tangible property is any property that can be seen or touched. Intangible property is property, such as a copyright or franchise, that is not tangible. Depreciable property may be real or personal. Personal property is property, such as machinery or equipment, that is not real estate. Real property is land and generally anything that is erected on, growing on, or attached to land. However, land itself is never depreciable.

FIGURING DEPRECIATION

Before figuring depreciation deductions, you must know:

1. What your basis in the property is;
2. When the property was placed in service; and
3. Which method of depreciation you are permitted to use.

Basis is a measure of your investment in the property you own. When you depreciate property, a certain percentage of your basis in it is deducted each year.

For property that you buy, your original basis is usually its cost to you. For property that you acquire in some other way—such as by inheriting it, receiving it as a gift, building it yourself, or getting it in a tax-free exchange—you must figure your original basis in some other way.

Accelerated Cost Recovery System (ACRS)

Most property that you place in service after 1980 is recovery property. Recovery property is tangible property of a character subject to the allowance for depreciation. You figure your depreciation deductions for recovery property under ACRS, the accelerated cost recovery system. ACRS applies equally to both new and used recovery property.

However, you cannot use ACRS for property you placed in service before 1981. ACRS also cannot be used for intangible depreciable property, or for tangible property that is acquired in certain types of transactions. See Excluded Property, later.

RECOVERY PERIODS

Under ACRS, tangible recovery property that you place in service after 1980 is depreciated over a period of 3, 5, 10, 15, 18, or 19 years, depending on the type of property.

1. 3-year property. This class includes personal property with a short useful life, such as automobiles, tractor units for use over the road, and light-duty trucks.
2. 5-year property. This class includes personal property that is not 3-year property. It includes most equipment.
3. 10-year property. This class includes certain real property such as certain public utility property and theme park structures. Manufactured homes, including mobile homes, are also designated as 10-year property.
4. 15-year property. This class includes all real property placed in service before March 16, 1984, such as

buildings, other than any designated as 10-year property. It also includes low-income housing.

5. 18-year property. This class includes real property, other than any designated as 10-year property, placed in service after March 15, 1984, and before May 9, 1985.
6. 19-year property. This class includes real property, other than any designated as 10-year property, placed in service after May 8, 1985.

See Publication 534 for a discussion of the transition rules for 15-, 18-, and 19-year property.

FIGURING ACRS DEDUCTIONS

The deduction under ACRS is figured by multiplying your "unadjusted" basis (explained later) in the property by a certain percentage. This percentage varies from year to year during the recovery period. For 3-, 5-, and 10-year property, the full first-year percentage applies no matter when in the tax year the property is placed in service.

The percentages for 3-, 5-, and 10-year recovery property are:

3-year property:

1st year	25%
2nd year	38%
3rd year	37%

5-year property:

1st year	15%
2nd year	22%
3rd through 5th year	21%

10-year property:

1st year	8%
2nd year	14%
3rd year	12%

4th through 6th year........................10%
7th through 10th year.......................9%

The percentages for 15-, 18-, and 19-year real property depend on when you place the property in service during your tax year. The tables below show the percentages for the first 6 years of the 15-year recovery period and the first 4 years of the 18-year recovery period. Find the month that you placed the property in service and use the percentages listed under that month for your depreciation deduction. For the percentages that apply to 18-year real property placed in service after March 15 and before June 23, 1984, 19-year real property, and low-income housing projects, see Publication 534.

15-year Real Property (other than low-income housing)

	Use the column for the month placed in service											
Year	1	2	3	4	5	6	7	8	9	10	11	12
1st	12%	11%	10%	9%	8%	7%	6%	5%	4%	3%	2%	1%
2nd	10%	10%	11%	11%	11%	11%	11%	11%	11%	11%	11%	12%
3rd	9%	9%	9%	9%	10%	10%	10%	10%	10%	10%	10%	10%
4th	8%	8%	8%	8%	8%	8%	9%	9%	9%	9%	9%	9%
5th	7%	7%	7%	7%	7%	7%	8%	8%	8%	8%	8%	8%
6th	6%	6%	6%	6%	7%	7%	7%	7%	7%	7%	7%	7%

18-year Real Property (placed in service after June 22, 1984)

Year	1	2	3	4	5	6	7	8	9	10	11	12
1st	9%	9%	8%	7%	6%	5%	4%	4%	3%	2%	1%	0.4%
2nd	9%	9%	9%	9%	9%	9%	9%	9%	9%	10%	10%	10%
3rd	8%	8%	8%	8%	8%	8%	8%	8%	9%	9%	9%	9%
4th	7%	7%	7%	7%	7%	8%	8%	8%	8%	8%	8%	8%

Note: Complete tables are in Publication 534.

UNADJUSTED BASIS

You figure the ACRS deduction by multiplying your unadjusted basis in the property by the applicable percentage for the year. Unadjusted basis is the same amount you would use to compute a gain on a sale with no adjustment for any depreciation, but reduced by the amount you properly amortize, by the amount you elect to deduct, and by 50 percent of the investment credit.

Example. You purchased and placed in service an apartment building on March 1,1984. Your adjusted basis in the building is $250,000 and you use the calendar year as your tax year. The building is 15-year real property, since it was placed in service before March 16, 1984. March is the 3rd month of your tax year. Your ACRS deduction for 1984 was 10 percent of $250,000, or $25,000. For 1985, the percentage for the 3rd month of the 2nd year of the recovery period is 11 percent. Therefore, your deduction is 11 percent of $250,000, or $27,500. For the 3rd and 4th years of the recovery period (1986 and 1987), the percentages are 9 percent and 8 percent.

Excluded Property

There are three rules that keep a person from using ACRS for certain property originally placed in service before 1981 but transferred after 1980. For property acquired after 1980, you must use another method of figuring your depreciation deductions if these special rules apply.

PERSONAL PROPERTY

You may not use ACRS for personal property you acquire after 1980 if any of the following three conditions apply:

1. You or a party related to you owned or used the property in 1980.
2. You lease the property to a person who owned or used the property in 1980.
3. You acquire the property from its 1980 owner, but the person who is actually using the property does not change.

REAL PROPERTY

You may not use ACRS for real property you acquire after 1980 if either of the following conditions apply:

1. You or a party related to you owned the property during 1980.
2. You lease the property back to its 1980 owner or a party related to its 1980 owner.

Related Parties. For the preceding rules, a party related to you includes members of the immediate family (including husband and wife), ancestors, or lineal descendants.

These rules also apply to certain relationships between individuals, corporations, partners, partnerships, and fiduciaries. However, these rules do not apply to property inherited after 1980 if your basis is the fair market value at the date of the decedent's death or the alternate valuation date.

For more information on excluded property, see Publication 534.

Other Depreciation Methods

Before ACRS was enacted, several other methods were used to figure depreciation. If you placed your property in service before 1981, or if your property does not qualify for ACRS, you must still use these methods for property that qualifies for ACRS.

These methods differ from ACRS in three ways:

1. Useful life. Instead of taking depreciation deductions over a specified recovery period, you take them over the useful life of the property.
2. First year. Instead of figuring your deduction for the first year using the percentages in the tables or the half-year convention, you must first figure the deduction that would be allowed for a full year and then prorate it for the part of the year you actually have the

property in service. You can only depreciate property for the part of the year it is in service or available for service.

3. Salvage value. You must take salvage value into account when figuring depreciation.

Salvage value is the estimated value of property at the end of its useful life. It is what you expect you will get from the sale or other disposition of the property when you no longer use it.

However, if you acquire personal property that has a useful life of three years or more, you may use an amount for salvage value that is less than your actual estimate. You may lower your estimate of salvage value by up to 10 percent of the property's adjusted basis. If your estimate is less than 10 percent of the adjusted basis, you may consider salvage value to be zero.

STRAIGHT-LINE METHOD

You may use this method for every kind of depreciable property.

To figure your deduction, you must determine the adjusted basis, salvage value, and useful life of the property. Subtract the salvage value, if any, from the adjusted basis and divide the amount by the number of years in useful life. This gives you the amount of depreciation you may deduct each year. This amount stays the same each year, unless the adjusted basis or useful life changes.

DECLINING BALANCE METHOD

Depending on the kind of property, you may use the 150 percent declining balance method or the 125 percent declining balance method.

To figure your deduction, first determine your rate of depreciation. This is generally determined by dividing the number 1 by the useful life. If the property had a useful life of 5 years, the rate of depreciation would be one-fifth, or 20 percent. This basic rate must be multiplied by the percentage allowed for the kind of property you are depreciating. Under the 150 percent declining balance method, the rate would be 30 percent (20% × 1.5).

Multiply the adjusted basis by this rate to figure your depreciation for the first year. If the declining balance rate was 30 percent and the adjusted basis was $2,000, the depreciation would be $600 ($2,000 × 30%). In the second year, first adjust your basis for the amount of depreciation you took the year before. Your adjusted basis would now be $1,400 ($2,000 – $600). Then multiply the adjusted basis by the same rate of depreciation you used in the first year (30 percent). This gives you a depreciation deduction for the second year of $420 ($1,400 × .30).

You may use the 150 percent declining balance method for used tangible personal property, such as a used machine, truck, or car used for business. The property must have a useful life of three years or more.

You may use the 125 percent declining balance method for certain used residential rental property. The property must have a useful life of 20 years or more. You must use the straight-line method for other used real estate. See Publication 534 for a discussion of residential rental property.

SALVAGE VALUE

Under the declining balance method, you do not reduce the adjusted basis by the salvage value before figuring the depreciation. However, you may not depreciate property below a reasonable salvage value.

CHANGE IN METHOD OF DEPRECIATION

For certain changes in method of depreciation, you must request permission from the Internal Revenue Service. To do this, file Form 3115, Application for Change in Accounting Method.

You may change from the declining balance method to the straight-line method without permission if you do not have a written agreement with the Internal Revenue Service that prohibits that change. For more information on changes in method of depreciation and what information is required when filing Form 3115, see Publication 534.

For more information on depreciation, ACRS, and the new rules, see Publication 534.

Glossary

Abandonment. The voluntary relinquishment of rights of ownership or another form of interest (an easement) by failure to use the property over an extended period of time.
Abstract of Title. A summary of the conveyances, transfers, and any other data relied on as evidence of title, together with any other elements of record that may impair the title. Still in use in some states, but giving way to the use of title insurance.
Accelerated Depreciation. Depreciation in which deductions in the first years are larger than deductions in the later years. This form of depreciation is usually used for income tax purposes.
Acceleration Clause. A clause in a mortgage or deed of trust giving the lender the right to call all monies owed to be immediately due and payable upon the happening of a certain stated event.
Acceptance. A legal term denoting acceptance of an offer. A buyer offers to buy, and the seller accepts the offer.
Access Right. A right to enter and exit one's property.
Acknowledgment. A formal declaration before an authorized official (usually a notary public) by a person who has executed (signed) a document, that he did in fact execute the document.

Agency Agreement (Listing). A listing agreement between the seller of real property and a broker, wherein the broker's commission is protected against a sale by other agents but not by the principal (seller). Often referred to as a nonexclusive agency listing.

Agreement of Sale. A written contract between the buyer and the seller, where both parties fully agree on the terms and conditions of the sale.

Alienation Clause. A clause within a loan instrument calling for payment of a debt in its entirety when ownership of the secured property is transferred. Also called a "due-on-sale" clause.

All-Inclusive Deed of Trust. *See* Wraparound Mortgage.

ALTA (American Land Title Association). A group of title insurance companies that issues title insurance to lenders.

Amenities. Attractive or desirable improvements to property, such as a pool or view.

Amortization. The liquidation of a financial obligation using regular equal payments on an installment basis.

Appraisal. An estimate and opinion of value; a factual conclusion resulting from an analysis of pertinent data.

Appreciation. Increase in value of property from improvements or the elimination of negative factors.

Assemblage. Process of acquiring contiguous properties into one overall parcel for a specific use or to increase the value of the whole.

Assessed Value. Value placed on property by the tax assessor.

Assessor. One appointed to assess property for taxation.

Assignee. One who receives an assignment.

Assignment. A transfer or making over to another the whole of any property, real or personal, or of any estate or right therein. To assign is to transfer.

Assignor. One who owns property assigned.

Assumption of Mortgage. The agreement of a buyer to assume the liability of an existing mortgage. Normally, the lender has to approve the new debtor before the existing debtor is released from the liability. (Exceptions to this generally arise with VA and FHA loans.)

Attachment. Seizure of property by court order, usually done in a pending lawsuit to make property available in case of judgment.

Balance Sheet. A financial statement that shows true condition of a business as of a particular date. Discloses assets, liabilities, and net worth.

Balloon Payment. The final installment paid at the end of the term of a note; used only when preceding installments were insufficient to pay off the note in full.

Bankruptcy. Procedure of federal law to seize the property of a debtor and divide it among his creditors.

Beneficiary. The lender involved in a note and deed of trust. One entitled to the benefit of a trust.

Bequeath. To give or leave personal property by a will.

Bill of Sale. An instrument used to transfer personal property.

Bond. An insurance agreement by which one party is insured against loss or default by a third party. In the construction business, a performance bond ensures the interested party that the contractor will complete the project. A bond can also be a method of financing debt by a government or corporation; such an instrument is interest-bearing and has priority over stock in terms of security.

Book Value. The value of an asset plus improvements less depreciation.

Boot. A term used when trading property. Boot is the additional value given in order to equalize values.

Breach. Violation of an obligation in a contract.

Broker, Real Estate. An agent licensed by the state to carry on the business of operating in real estate. A broker usually receives a commission for the services of bringing together buyers and sellers, owners and tenants, in exchange agreements

Building Code. A set of stringent laws that control the construction of buildings, design, materials, and other similar factors.

Building Line. A line set by law or deed a certain distance from the street line, in front of which an owner cannot build on his lot. Also known as a setback line.

Built-ins. Items that are not movable, such as stoves, ovens, microwave ovens, dishwashers.

Business Opportunity. The sale or lease of a business and goodwill of an existing business enterprise.

Buyers' Market. In residential real estate, a market condition in which more homes are for sale than there are interested buyers.

Capital Gain. For income tax purposes, the gain realized from the sale of an asset less the purchase price and deductible expenses.

Capitalization. An appraising term used in determining value by considering net operating income and a percentage of reasonable return on investment.

Capitalization Rate. A percentage used by an investor to determine the value of income property through capitalization.

Cash Flow. The owner's spendable income after deducting operating expenses and debt service.

Chain of Title. A history of conveyances and encumbrances affecting the title as far back as records are available.

Client. One who employs the services of another, such as an attorney, real estate agent, or insurance agent.

Closing. In the sale of real estate, the final moment when all documents are executed and recorded and the sale is complete. Also a general selling term for the process in which a salesperson is attempting to sell something and the buyer agrees to purchase.

Closing Costs. Incidental expenses incurred with the sale of real estate, such as appraisal fees, loan fees, and termite report.

Closing Statement. A list of the final accounting of all monies of both buyer and seller prepared by an escrow agent; notes all costs each must pay at the completion of a real estate transaction.

Cloud on Title. An encumbrance on real property which affects the rights of the owner; often keeps the title from being marketable until the cloud is removed.

Collateral Security. A separate obligation attached to another contract pledging something of value to guarantee performance of the contract.

Common Area. That area owned in common by owners of condominiums and planned unit development homes within a subdivision.

Compound Interest. Interest paid on the original principal and on interest accrued.

Condemnation. A declaration by governing powers that a structure is unfit for use.

Conditional Sales Contract. A contract for the sale of property where the buyer has possession and use but the seller retains title until the conditions of the contract have been fulfilled. Also known as a land contract.

Condominium. A system of individual ownership of units in a multi-unit structure where each space is individually owned but each owner jointly owns the common areas and the land.

Conformity, Principle of. An appraising term stating that uniformity throughout a certain area produces highest value.
Conservator. A court-appointed guardian.
Construction Loan. The short-term financing of improvements on real estate. Once the improvements are completed, a take-out loan for a longer term is usually issued.
Contingency. A condition upon which a valid contract is dependent. For example, the sale of a house is contingent upon the buyer obtaining adequate financing.
Contract. An agreement between two or more parties, written or oral, to do or not to do certain things.
Contract of Sale. Same as a conditional sales contract or a land contract.
Conventional Loan. A loan, usually on real estate, that is not backed by the federal government through FHA or VA.
Conveyance. The transfer of the title to land from one to another.
Cooperative. A building with two or more units in which the right to live is acquired by the purchase of stock in a corporation that owns the property. This form of real property was a forerunner to the condominium and is less popular due to difficulty in financing because there is no individual ownership of each unit.
Cost Approach. A method of appraisal in which the structure's estimated cost is calculated less the land value and depreciation.
Counteroffer. An offer in response to an offer. *A* offers $60,000 for *B*'s house, which is listed for $62,000. *B* counteroffers *A*'s offer by stating that he will sell the house to *A* for $61,000. The $61,000 is a counteroffer.
Covenants. Agreements written into deeds and other instruments stating performance or nonperformance of certain acts or noting certain uses or nonuses of the property.
CPM. Certified Property Manager.
CRV (Certificate of Reasonable Value). An appraisal of real property by the Veterans Administration.
Current Assets. An accounting term representing assets that can readily be converted into cash, as with stocks and short-term accounts receivable.
Current Liabilities. Short-term debts.
Deed. A written instrument that, when executed, conveys title or real property.

Default. Failure to fulfill or discharge an obligation, or to perform any act that has been agreed to in writing.
Deferred Payments. Payments to begin in the future.
Delivery. The placing of property in the possession of the grantee.
Demise. A lease or conveyance to another for life or years, or an estate at will.
Demographics. Statistics describing human populations.
Density. The amount of crowding together of buildings, people, or other things.
Depletion. The reduction or loss in value of an asset.
Deposit Receipt. The form used to accept the earnest money deposit to secure the offer for the purchase of real estate.
Depreciation. Loss of value of an asset brought about by age (physical deterioration), or functional and economic obsolescence. Percentage reduction of property value year-by-year for tax purposes.
Depression. That part of a business cycle where unemployment is high, and production and overall purchasing by the public are low. A severe recession.
Devise. A gift of real estate by will.
Diminishing Returns. An economic theory that states an increase in capital or manpower will not increase production proportionately (four laborers may do less than four times the work of one laborer; and two laborers may do more than twice the work of one laborer). The return diminishes when production is proportionately less than the input.
Directional Growth. The path of development of an urban area. Used to determine where future development will be most profitable.
Divided Interest. Different interest in the same property, such as interest of the owner, lessee, or mortgagee.
Documentary Tax Stamps. Stamps affixed to a deed denoting the amount of transfer tax paid.
Domicile. The place where a person has a permanent home.
Double Declining Method of Depreciation. An accelerated method of depreciating an asset where double the amount of straight-line depreciation is deducted from the balance.
Down Payment. Cash paid toward a purchase by the buyer, as opposed to the amount financed.

Easement. The right to use another person's land for a specific purpose.
Economic Life. The period over which a property will yield a return on the investment.
Economic Obsolescence. Loss of useful life and desirability of a property through economic forces, such as a change in zoning or traffic flow, rather than deterioration.
Economic Rent. The current market rental rate based on comparable rent paid for a similar unit.
Effective Age. The age of a structure estimated by its condition as opposed to its actual age.
Eminent Domain. The right of the government to acquire private property for public use by condemnation. The owner must be fully compensated.
Encroachment. Trespass. The building of any improvements partly or wholly on the property of another.
Encumbrance. Anything that affects or limits the fee simple title to property, such as mortgages, trust deeds, easements, or restrictions of any kind. Liens are special encumbrances that make the property security for a debt.
Entity. An existence or being, as in a corporation or business, rather than an individual.
Equity. The value an owner has in property over and above the liens against it. A legal term based on fairness, rather than strict interpretation of the law.
Equity Buildup. The reduction in the difference between property value and the amount of the lien as regular payments are made. The equity increases (builds up) on an amortized loan as the proportion of interest payment reduces, causing the amount going toward principal to increase.
Escalation Clause. A clause in a lease providing for an increased rent at a future time due to increased costs to the lessor, such as a rise in the cost of living index or a tax increase.
Escrow. A neutral third party who carries out the provisions of an agreement between two parties.
Estate. The ownership interest of a person in real property. A deceased person's property. A large home with spacious grounds.
Exclusive-Right-to-Sell Listing. A written contract between agent and owner where the agent has the right to collect a commission if the property is sold by anyone during the term of the agreement.

Executor. The person appointed in a will to carry out the terms of the will.

Face Value. The value stated on the face of notes, mortgages, etc., without consideration of any discounting.

Fair Market Value. The price a property will bring if buyer and seller are both fully aware of market conditions and comparable properties.

Federal Deposit Insurance Corporation (FDIC). The federal corporation that insures bank depositors against loss up to a specified amount (currently $100,000).

Federal Home Loan Bank Board. The board that charters and regulates federal savings and loan associations and Federal Home Loan Banks.

Federal Home Loan Banks. Regulated by the Federal Home Loan Bank Board. Currently 12 regional branches where banks, savings and loans, insurance companies, or similar institutions may join the system and borrow for the purpose of making available a permanent supply of home financing money.

Federal Savings and Loan Insurance Corporation (FSLIC). A federal corporation that insures deposits in savings and loan associations up to a specified amount (currently $100,000).

Fee Simple. Ownership of title to property without any limitation; can be sold, left at will, or inherited.

FHA (Federal Housing Administration). The federal agency that insures first mortgages on homes, enabling lenders to extend more lenient terms to homeowners.

FHLMC (Freddie Mac). Federal Home Loan Mortgage Corporation. A federal agency that purchases first mortgages from members of the Federal Reserve System and the Federal Home Loan Bank System.

Fiduciary. A person in a position of trust and confidence, as between principal and broker; the broker as a fiduciary owes the principal loyalty, which cannot be breached under rules of agency.

First Mortgage. A mortgage having priority over all other voluntary liens against a specific property.

Fixtures. Items affixed to buildings or land usually in such a way that they cannot be moved without damage to themselves or the property, such as plumbing, electrical fixtures, and trees.

FNMA (Fannie Mae). Federal National Mortgage Association. A private corporation that purchases first mortgages at discounts.

Foreclosure. Procedure where property pledged for security for a debt is sold to pay the debt in the event of default in payment and terms.

Front Footage. The linear measurement along the front of a parcel. That portion of the parcel which fronts the street or walkway.

Functional Obsolescence. Loss in value due to out-of-date or poorly designed equipment.

GNMA (Ginnie Mae). Government National Mortgage Association. Purchases first mortgages at discounts, similarly to FNMA.

Graduated Lease. A lease that provides for rental adjustments, often based upon future determination of the cost of living index; used for the most part in long-term leases.

Grant. To transfer an interest in real property, such as an easement.

Gross Income. Total scheduled income from property before any expenses are deducted.

Gross Income Multiplier. An appraising rule of thumb; when multiplied by the annual gross income of a property, will estimate the market value.

Gross Lease. A lease obligating the lessor to pay all or part of the expenses incurred on leased property.

Ground Lease. A lease of vacant land.

Ground Rent. Rent paid for vacant land.

Highest and Best Use. An appraisal term for the use of land that will bring the highest economic return over a given time.

Homeowners' Association. An association of homeowners within a community formed to improve and maintain the quality of the community. An association formed by the developer of condominiums or planned developments.

Homestead. A declaration by the owner of a home that protects the home against judgments up to specified amounts provided by certain state laws.

Impound Account. A trust account held for the purpose of paying taxes, insurance, and other periodic expenses incurred for real property.

Improvements. A general term to describe buildings, roads, and utilities that have been added to raw (unimproved) land.

Inflation. The increase in the supply of money, which reduces its purchasing power. Usually identified with rapidly increasing prices.

Installment Note. A note that provides for regular monthly payments to be paid on the date specified in the instrument.

Instrument. A written legal document.

Intangible Value. The goodwill or well-advertised name of an established business.

Interim Loan. A short-term loan usually for real estate improvements during the period of construction.

Intestate. The condition of dying without having made a will.

Intrinsic Value. The value of a thing in the absence of certain aspects that will add value to some and not to others; for example, a vintage Rolls-Royce might have value to a car collector, but to anyone else it might not.

Investment. The putting up of money with the intent of making a profit.

Joint Tenancy. Joint ownership by two or more persons with right of survivorship. Upon death, a joint tenant's interest does not go to his heirs, but to the remaining joint tenants.

Junior Mortgage. A mortgage that is lower in priority than a first mortgage.

Land Contract. A contract for the sale of property where the buyer has possession and use, but the seller retains title until the conditions of the contract have been fulfilled. Same as a conditional sales contract.

Land Grant. A gift of public land by the federal government.

Lease. A contract between the owner of real property, called the lessor, and another person, referred to as the lessee, covering the conditions by which the lessee may occupy and use the property.

Lease Option. A lease in which the lessee has the option to purchase the leased property. The terms of the option must be set forth in the lease.

Legacy. A gift of personal property by will.

Legal Description. The geographical identification of a parcel of land.

Lessee. One who contracts to rent property under a specified lease.

Lessor. An owner who contracts into a lease with a tenant (lessee).

Leverage. The use of a small amount of value to control a much larger amount of value.

Liability. A term covering all types of debts and obligations.

Lien. An encumbrance against real property for money, including taxes, mortgages, and judgments.

Limited Partnership. A partnership of one or more general partners, who operate the business, along with one or more limited partners, who contribute capital but are liable only up to the amount of money contributed.

Liquidation. Disposal of property or assets; the settlement of debts.

Lis Pendens. A recorded legal notice showing pending litigation of real property. Anyone acquiring an interest in such property after the recording of "lis pendens" could be bound to the outcome of the litigation.

Listing. A contract between owner and broker to sell the owner's property.

Long-Term Capital Gain. Gain on the sale of property that was held for at least six months.

Maintenance Reserve. Money held in reserve to cover anticipated maintenance expenses.

Market Data Approach. An appraisal method to determine value by comparing similar properties with the subject property.

Market Value. The price a buyer will pay and a seller will accept, both being fully informed of market conditions.

Master Plan. A comprehensive zoning plan to allow a city to grow in an orderly manner.

Mechanic's Lien. A lien created by statute on a specific property for labor or materials contributed to an improvement on that property.

Metes and Bounds. A form of legal description.

MGIC (Mortgage Guaranty Insurance Corporation). Private corporation that insures mortgage loans.

Moratorium. Temporary suspension of the enforcement of liability for a debt.

Mortgage. An instrument by which property is hypothecated to secure the payment of a debt.

Mortgage Broker. A person who, for a fee, brings together the lender with the borrower. Also known as a loan broker.

Multiple Listing. A listing taken by a member of an organization of brokers, whereby all members have an opportunity to find a buyer.

Net Income. Gross income less operating expenses.

Net Lease. A lease requiring the tenant to pay all or part of the expenses on leased property in addition to the stipulated rent.

Net Listing. A listing in which the agent may retain as compensation all sums received over and above a net price to the owner. Illegal in many states.

Net Worth. Total assets less liabilities.

Nonexclusive Listing. A listing in which the agent has an exclusive listing with respect to other agents, but the owner may sell the property without being liable for a commission.

Notary Public. One who is authorized by federal or local government to attest authentic signatures and administer oaths.

Note. A written instrument acknowledging a debt and promising payment.

Offer. A presentation to form a contract or agreement.

Open Listing. An authorization given by an owner to a real estate agent to sell the owner's property. Open listings may be given to more than one agent without liability, but only the one who secures a buyer on satisfactory terms receives a commission.

Operating Expenses. Expenses relevant to income-producing property, such as taxes, management, utilities, insurance, and other day-to-day costs.

Option. A right given, for consideration, to purchase or lease property upon stipulated terms within a specific period of time.

Percentage Lease. A lease on property where a minimum specified rent is paid or a percentage of gross receipts of the lessee is paid, whichever is higher.

Personal Property. Property that is not real property (real estate).

Planned Development. Five or more individually owned lots where one or more other parcels are owned in common or there are reciprocal rights in one or more other parcels. A subdivision.

Plat (Plat Map). A map or plan of a specified parcel of land.

PMI (Private Mortgage Insurance). Insurance that covers a portion of the first mortgage, allowing the lender to offer more lenient terms to a borrower.

Point. One percent. A fee stated in points is often charged by the lender to originate the loan. On VA and many FHA loans, the seller pays points to accommodate the loan.

Prepayment Penalty. A penalty within a note, mortgage, or deed of trust imposing a penalty if the debt is paid in full before the end of its term.

Prime Lending Rate. The most favorable interest rate charged by a bank to its biggest customers.

Principal. The employer of an agent. The amount of debt, not including interest.

Proration. To divide equally or proportionately to time of use.

Purchase Agreement. An agreement between buyer and seller denoting price and terms of the sale.

Pyramid. To build an estate by multiple acquisitions of properties, using the initial properties as a base for further investment.

Realtor. A real estate broker holding membership in a real estate board affiliated with the National Association of Realtors.

Redemption. The repurchase of one's property after it has been lost through foreclosure. Payment of delinquent taxes after sale to the state.

REIT (Real Estate Investment Trust). A method of group investment with certain tax advantages, governed by federal and state laws.

Rent. Consideration, usually money, for the occupancy and use of property.

Replacement Cost Method. A method of appraisal to determine value by estimating the cost to build an exact replica.

Request for Notice of Default. A request by a lender, which is recorded for notification, in the case of default by a loan with priority.

Riparian Rights. A landowner's rights to water on, under, or adjacent to his land.

Sale-Leaseback. A sale in which the buyer subsequently leases the property back to the seller.

Secondary Financing. A junior loan or a loan second in priority to a first mortgage or deed of trust.

Security Deposit. Money given to a landlord by the tenant to secure performance of the rental agreement.

Sellers' Market. A market in which there are more buyers than sellers.

Severalty. An estate held by one person alone.

Sheriff's Deed. Deed given by court order in connection with the sale of a property to satisfy a judgment.

Single-Family Residence. A general term to distinguish a house from an apartment building, a condominium, or a planned unit development.

Special Assessment. Legal charge against real estate by a public authority to pay the cost of public improvements (such as sewers) by which the property is benefited.

Speculator. One who buys property with the intent of selling quickly at a profit.

Spendable Income. Net income after taxes.

SRA (Society of Real Estate Appraisers). Designation given to those who have achieved certain experience and education in the field of appraising.

Straight-Line Depreciation. Reducing the value for accounting purposes over an extended period by equal increments.

Straight Note. A nonamortized note promising to repay a loan, and including the amount, term, and interest rate.

Subdivision. A division of one parcel of land into smaller lots.

Subject to Mortgage. A buyer who takes title to real property "subject to mortgage" is not responsible to the holder of the note. The original maker of the note is not released from the responsibility of the note, and the most the buyer can lose in foreclosure is his equity in the property.

Sublease. A lease given by a lessee.

Syndicate. A group of investors who invest in one or more properties through a partnership, corporation, or trust.

Take-Out Commitment. Agreement by a lender to have available a long-term loan over a specified time once construction is completed.

Tax Sale. A sale of property, usually at auction, for nonpayment of taxes assessed against it.

Tenancy in Common. Ownership by two or more persons who hold an undivided interest without right of survivorship.

Tenant. The holder of real property under a rental agreement.

Tenements. All rights in land that pass with the conveyance of the land. Also commonly refers to certain groups of multiple dwellings.

Testator. A person who leaves a valid will at death.
Title Insurance. Insurance written by a title company to protect the property owner against loss if title is imperfect.
Township. A territorial subdivision 6 miles long, 6 miles wide, and containing 36 sections, each 1 mile square.
Tract House. A house similar to other homes within a subdivision and built by the same developer, as opposed to a custom home built to owner specifications.
Trade Fixtures. A business's personal property that is attached to the real property but can be removed upon the sale of the real estate.
Trust Deed. An instrument that conveys legal title of a property to a trustee to be held pending fulfillment of an obligation, usually the repayment of a loan to a beneficiary (lender).
Trustee. One who holds bare legal title to a property in trust for another to secure performance of an obligation.
Trustor. The borrower of money secured by a deed of trust.
Unimproved Land. Land in its natural state without structures on it.
Unlawful Detainer. An action of law to evict a person or persons occupying real property unlawfully.
Usury. Interest rate on a loan in excess of that permitted by law.
Variable Interest Rate. A fluctuating interest rate that can go up or down depending on the going market rate.
Vendee. A purchaser or buyer.
Vendor. A seller.
Vested. Bestowed upon someone or secured by someone.
Voluntary Lien. A lien, such as a mortgage, that is made at the owner's choice.
Waive. To relinquish or abandon. To forgo a right to enforce or require anything.
Wraparound Mortgage. A second mortgage that is subordinate to but includes the face value of the first mortgage.
Zoning. Act of city or county authorities specifying the permitted uses of properties in specific areas.

Index